Contents

Events in the Life of Harriet Tubman

The exact dates of many of the events in Harriet Tubman's life, including her birthday, are unknown.

1820 or 1822
Araminta "Minty" Ross, later known as Harriet Tubman, is born in Dorchester County, Maryland, probably in February or March, to Harriet "Rit" Green and Ben Ross.

1825
Edward Brodess sells Mariah Ritty, Minty's older sister.

Approximately 1830
To avoid a whipping, Minty runs away for the first time. She hides in a pigsty until hunger forces her to go back to her master.

1844
Minty marries free man John Tubman. It is believed that on her wedding day, she may have changed her name from Araminta to Harriet.

October 1849
Minty runs away by herself, and with help from the Underground Railroad, reaches Pennsylvania—a Free State—and finds freedom.

1851–1857
Harriet leads many slaves to freedom using the Underground Railroad. Her sister Rachel remains in slavery, although Harriet tries to rescue her many times.

Fall 1860
Learning that Rachel has died, Harriet leads the Ennals family north. It is her last rescue.

June 1, 1863
Tubman becomes the first American woman to lead an armed raid in battle. She frees more than 750 slaves.

September 30, 1867
Harriet's husband, John Tubman, is murdered in Cambridge, Maryland. Harriet finds out about this in October.

March 18, 1869
Harriet marries Nelson Davis at the Central Presbyterian Church in Auburn, New York.

1886
A new edition of Harriet's biography, *Harriet, the Moses of Her People*, is published.

Spring 1896
Harriet buys land to build a home for elderly and sick African Americans.

March 10, 1913
Harriet Tubman dies and is buried with military honors.

March 2, 1824
Edward Brodess, Minty's owner, marries Eliza Ann Keene. Minty and the rest of her family are separated from their father and moved to Edward Brodess's plantation.

Approximately 1828
Minty is hired out to James Cook, the first of many masters.

Approximately 1836
Minty is hit in the head by a lead weight and almost dies.

September 17, 1849
Following the death of Edward Brodess, Harriet fears she is about to be sold, and she runs away with her brothers, but they force her to turn back.

December 1850
After the Fugitive Slave Act, or the Bloodhound Law, is passed in September, Harriet conducts her first rescue by helping her niece Kessiah and her children escape.

May–July 1857
Harriet leads her parents out of Maryland and into St. Catharines, Canada.

April 12, 1861
Confederate forces open fire on Fort Sumter, South Carolina, and the Civil War begins. Tubman soon becomes a nurse, scout, and spy for the Union.

April 9, 1865
The Civil War ends. On her way home to Auburn, New York, Harriet is injured by a train conductor who forces her to leave her seat.

December 1868
Sarah Bradford publishes *Scenes in the Life of Harriet Tubman*.

September 1873
Harriet is tricked out of $2,000 by men claiming to have Confederate gold.

October 18, 1888
Harriet's second husband, Nelson Davis, dies, probably of tuberculosis.

June 23, 1908
The Harriet Tubman Home is opened by the AME Zion Church.

STERLING BIOGRAPHIES

HARRIET TUBMAN

Leading the Way to Freedom

Laurie Calkhoven

STERLING

New York / London
www.sterlingpublishing.com/kids

For Derek, Brandon, Nicole, and Kendra with love

STERLING and the distinctive Sterling logo are registered trademarks of
Sterling Publishing Co., Inc.

Library of Congress Cataloging-in-Publication Data

Calkhoven, Laurie.
    Harriet Tubman : leading the way to freedom / Laurie Calkhoven.
        p. cm. -- (Sterling biography)
    Includes bibliographical references and index.
    ISBN-13: 978-1-4027-4117-3
    ISBN-10: 1-4027-4117-0
    1. Tubman, Harriet, 1820?-1913--Juvenile literature. 2. Slaves--United States--
Biography--Juvenile literature. 3. African American women--Biography--Juvenile lit-
erature. 4. Underground Railroad--Juvenile literature. 5. Antislavery movements--
United States--History--19th century--Juvenile literature. I. Title.
    E444.T82C35 2008
    973.7'115092--dc22
    [B]
                                        2007019283

10 9 8 7 6 5 4 3 2 1

Published by Sterling Publishing Co., Inc
387 Park Avenue South, New York, NY 1
© 2008 by Laurie Calkhoven
Distributed in Canada by Sterling Publish
c/o Canadian Manda Group, 165 Dufferin
Toronto, Ontario, Canada M6K 3H6
Distributed in the United Kingdom by G
Castle Place, 166 High Street, Lewes, Eas
Distributed in Australia by Capricorn Lir
P.O. Box 704, Windsor, NSW 2756, Aust

Printed in China
All rights reserved

Sterling ISBN-13: 978-1-4027-4117-3 (paperback)
        ISBN-10: 1-4027-4117-0

Sterling ISBN-13: 978-1-4027-5800-3 (hardcover)
        ISBN-10: 1-4027-5800-6

Designed by Simonsays Design!
Image research by Larry Schwartz

For information about custom editions, special sales, premium and
corporate purchases, please contact Sterling Special Sales
Department at 800-805-5489 or specialsales@sterlingpub.com.

Freedom Fighter

If you are tired, keep going; if you are scared, keep going; if you are hungry, keep going; if you want to taste freedom, keep going.

Harriet Tubman crept into the woods on a dark night in 1849. She hid in swamps and forests and trusted strangers who could have betrayed her at any time—all in search of freedom. Born into slavery, she endured unimaginable hardships and ran away for the first time when she was just six. She finally made it to the North when she was in her twenties. Harriet then risked her liberty many times leading other slaves to freedom.

Harriet Tubman refused to be bound by chains of any kind, whether they were the real chains of slavery or the symbolic chains of **prejudice**. She went on to become a Civil War spy and a **suffragette**, fighting for freedom and equality for all people.

Whenever Harriet's passengers on the Underground Railroad got discouraged, she would say: "If you are tired, keep going; if you are scared, keep going; if you are hungry, keep going; if you want to taste freedom, keep going." There were many times when Harriet was tired, scared, and hungry, but she always kept going.

CHAPTER 1

Born into Slavery

I gave one jump out of the door, and I saw they came after me, but I just flew, and they didn't catch me.

Harriet Tubman was born Araminta "Minty" Ross in late February or early March in Dorchester County, Maryland. The year was 1820 or 1822, but no one knows for sure. Minty didn't know her birth date, so she never celebrated her birthday. Most slaves didn't. Slave owners didn't bother to record slave births, and slaves weren't taught to read or write, so they could not record their births, either. Teaching a slave to read was against the law.

Minty was born into slavery. Her earliest memories were of lying in a cradle made from a sweet gum tree. "I remember lying in that there, when the young ladies in the big house where my mother worked, come down, catch me up in the air before I could walk."

HARRIET TUBMAN
1820-1913

THE "MOSES OF HER PEOPLE." HARRIET TUBMAN OF THE BUCKTOWN DISTRICT FOUND FREEDOM FOR HERSELF AND SOME THREE HUNDRED OTHER SLAVES WHOM SHE LED NORTH. IN THE CIVIL WAR SHE SERVED THE UNION ARMY AS A NURSE, SCOUT AND SPY.

MARYLAND CIVIL WAR CENTENNIAL COMMISSION

A marker in Bucktown, Maryland, indicates the birthplace of Harriet Tubman and celebrates her fight for freedom.

Minty's father, Ben Ross, may have worked in a sawmill like the one shown in this engraving, c. 1870. Timber was one of Dorchester County's most important exports.

Though she was much too young to be a babysitter, she was left in charge of her younger brothers and sisters. "When I was four or five years old, my mother cooked up to the big house and left me to take care of the baby an' my little brother. I used to be in a hurry for her to go, so's I could play the baby was a pig in a bag." She took care of her baby brother "till he was so big I couldn't tote him any more."

One Family, Two Masters

Minty's mother, Harriet "Rit" Green, was also born into slavery. Before Minty was born, Rit was owned by Mary Pattison Brodess. When Mary's husband died, she married a local landowner named Anthony Thompson. Rit and any children she had would become the property of Mary's son Edward Brodess when he turned twenty-one. Until then, Mary's new husband would be Rit's master. One of Thompson's slaves, Ben Ross, managed the timber operations on Thompson's heavily forested property.

The family in this c. 1860 engraving is being divided and sold at auction. Slave families were constantly in danger of being separated forever.

Rit and Ben Ross met, married, and started a family around 1808. Like other slaves, Rit and Ben had to obtain both of their masters' permission to marry. Their family could be ripped apart at any time if Thompson changed his mind or decided to sell one of them or their children at a slave **auction**.

By the time Minty was born, the fifth of nine or eleven children, Mary Pattison Brodess had died and her son Edward Brodess was about to turn twenty-one. Rit and Ben must have worried about their family being divided, since Rit and her children were Edward's property, and Ben belonged to Anthony Thompson. If Edward claimed his own slaves and left his stepfather's home, the family would be separated. The Ross family's stable life would soon change.

Edward Brodess moved into his own home in 1823 or 1824 and later married Eliza Anne Keene. He took Rit and her children with him and became

… so now Minty and the rest of her family were separated from their father.

their new master. By that time, Minty's brother Ben and possibly her sister Rachel were born, so now Minty and the rest of her family were separated from their father.

Then, in 1825, Brodess did something even worse than splitting the family in two. Even though Rit had taken care of Edward when he was a baby and young child, he took one of Rit's children away from her. Brodess sold a slave named Rhody, who was probably Minty's older sister Mariah Ritty, to a slave trader from Mississippi, and Ritty was now forever lost to her mother and father.

The sale of Mariah Ritty and other slaves frightened Minty and her family. They felt they were always in danger of being separated.

A slave woman serves food to a plantation's black children behind the shacks they lived in. Black children were often fed as little as possible by their white owners.

Brodess owned more slaves than he needed. So he hired out his slaves to other landowners in exchange for money for himself, or food and clothing for the slaves. These slaves often had to travel great distances to work for temporary masters. Minty's mother was forced to spend a lot of time away from her children when they were very young, while she worked in the big house for Brodess or for other masters. Slaves worked from sunup to sundown six days a week, and slave children were left alone to take care of themselves. They were usually given as little food as possible.

Minty's First Job

By the time Minty was five or six, she was considered old enough to go to work and was hired out to a farmer named James Cook to learn the trade of weaving. Slave children often had no clothes, so they wore **gunnysacks** with holes cut in them for their heads and arms. Minty was excited when Eliza Brodess

Some slave owners and overseers believed their slaves wouldn't work unless they were regularly beaten. In this 1849 engraving, an overseer is shown whipping his slaves in the field.

Slave Quarters

On most **plantations**, slaves lived in a separate area away from the "big house" of their white owners. Slave quarters were often small, one-room shacks with dirt floors, little or no furniture, and almost no privacy. On some plantations, two or more families would share one small cabin.

On small farms without separate slave quarters, slaves slept on the kitchen floor, in the basement, or in the barn.

Slave quarters were often small and cramped, like these cabins in Port Royal, South Carolina.

made her a new dress for the journey. But that's where her excitement ended.

On the day she was supposed to leave, a man on horseback came to take her away from her mother. She was taken to the home of white people she did not know. Minty was scared and homesick. She had never been in such a house, having lived only in small slave cabins before. She was even embarrassed to eat in front of these new people. Minty would cry herself to sleep at night, lying on the floor in front of the fireplace.

Minty quickly discovered that James Cook and his wife were cruel. Minty was often beaten and treated like a piece of property rather than a human being. One of her jobs was to wade into the marsh with cold water up to her waist—to check her master's muskrat traps. Even when she was sick, she would be sent to do this job. Once, when Minty had the measles and was running a high fever, she became so ill that Cook thought she might die. A sick slave was useless to a slave master, so Cook brought the little girl back to Brodess.

Rit nursed Minty back to health, only to see her daughter sent back to the Cooks'. But Minty missed her mother, hated the Cooks, and would not learn to weave. Eventually she was sent home again, only to be hired out to another new master.

Slave Jobs

In the South, most slaves, both women and men, worked in tobacco, cotton, and rice fields. A few men on every plantation were taught to be carpenters, blacksmiths, road builders, or even lumbermen, like Harriet's father.

Some slaves were trained to work in the slave owner's home. They were known as house slaves. Women became maids, cooks, nurses, and laundresses. Men worked as butlers and valets who would tend to the personal care of their master.

House slaves generally had more privileges than field hands, but they also spent more time under their master's eye.

This 1863 engraving shows house slaves taking care of and entertaining the master's children. House slaves included maids, cooks, butlers, and nurses.

Minty's next job was as a nursemaid and house servant. The mistress, Miss Susan, gave her slaves enough food and clothing, but she believed that slaves wouldn't do their work unless they were regularly whipped. On Minty's first day, she was ordered to sweep the floors and dust the furniture. She tried to do her job well. She kept one eye on the whip on the mantel while she swept with all her strength. The minute she finished sweeping, she grabbed her dusting cloth and cleaned the furniture, and then left the room to set the breakfast table.

Minty had never been taught how to sweep and dust. She didn't know that the dust she stirred up with her broom settled on the furniture as soon as she finished dusting. Miss Susan didn't believe that Minty had done her work, so she grabbed the whip and beat the young girl on the head, face, and neck.

Another day Minty was whipped five times before breakfast. Her screams woke Miss Susan's sister Emily, who came to Minty's rescue and taught the young girl how to properly sweep and dust a room.

Dusting wasn't Minty's only chore in Miss Susan's house. Minty's workday was never ending, and at night she was forced to rock the baby's cradle. When the six- or seven-year-old Minty fell asleep after a long day of hard work, and the baby would start crying, Miss Susan, who slept with a whip under her pillow, would lash out at Minty. For the rest of her life, Minty had the scars from those painful beatings.

I Just Flew

It was the constant threat of beatings that led Minty to run away the first time. One morning, after breakfast, Minty stood behind Miss Susan waiting to take the baby. But Miss Susan began to argue with her husband. Minty had never tasted sugar before, and there was a bowl with lumps of sugar right next to her. She couldn't resist, and she quickly took one lump. But Miss Susan saw her and reached for the whip. "I gave one jump out of the door, and I saw they came after me, but I just flew, and they didn't catch me," Minty remembered years later.

Minty ran and ran, but she had no place to go. "I passed many a house, but I didn't dare to stop, for they all knew my Missus and they would send me back." Finally, she came to a pigpen with an old sow and eight or ten little pigs. Minty ran and tumbled inside with the pigs.

"I stayed from Friday till the next Tuesday, fighting with those little pigs for the potato peelings and other scraps that came down in the trough. The old sow would push me away when I tried to get her children's food, and I was awful afraid of her. By Tuesday I was so starved I knowed I'd got to go back to my Missus. I hadn't got no where else to go."

Minty knew what was coming. Only this time Miss Susan didn't whip her; Miss Susan's husband did.

Many years later, Minty's great nephew Harkless Bowley remembered her telling him of one beating that left her with pains in her side for the rest of her life. Minty's master crept up behind her while she worked and hit her over and over again with a rope that had a knot at one end. The beating broke her ribs and may have caused internal injuries. Half starved and unable to work, Minty was once again shipped back to Brodess.

Minty knew what was coming. Only this time Miss Susan didn't whip her; Miss Susan's husband did.

Beatings almost seemed like a way of life for Minty. But it did not break her spirit. One mistress whipped Minty every day, first

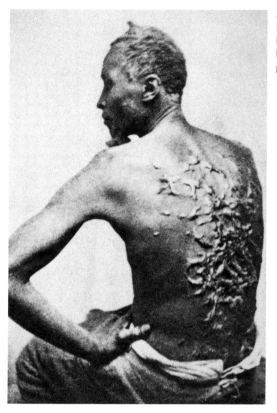

A freed slave from Louisiana displays his whip-scarred back in this 1863 photograph.

thing in the morning. But Minty learned to put on all of the thick clothes she could find as padding and yell her head off so the mistress would think that Minty was in terrible pain. Once, she bit another master on the knee, and he never whipped her again. She was often sickly and sent home. Rit would nurse her little girl back to health, but as soon as Minty was strong, Brodess would hire her out again.

"I grew up like a neglected weed," she said, many years later, "not happy or contented; every time I saw a white man I was afraid of being carried away."

A group of slaves, chained together to prevent escape, passes the unfinished Capitol building in Washington, D.C., c. 1820.

A Family's Heartbreak

Rit could protect her children only when they were with her, and even then, she was not always successful. Sometime during the 1830s, Brodess wanted money to buy more land. He sold Minty's sisters Linah and Soph. Linah was separated from her own two daughters. Because slaves could not read or write, there was no way to stay in touch with family members far away. Rit and Ben were not told what state their daughters were taken to. It was a heartbreaking moment for the entire family.

Years later, Minty said she never forgot her parents' terrible grief and the agonized looks on her sisters' faces, as they were led away weeping in a chain gang.

For a long time afterward, Minty was not able to close her eyes without seeing horsemen galloping toward her, and hearing the screams of women and children as they were dragged away to a life of slavery even worse than the one they had known in Maryland.

CHAPTER 2

An Almost Fatal Blow

[The weight] broke my skull and cut a piece of that shawl clean off and drove it into my head. They carried me to the house all bleeding and fainting.

Once again Minty was returned to Brodess, and he eventually gave up trying to turn her into a house slave. When she was around twelve years old, he put her to work in the fields. It was hard physical work, but Minty was happier outdoors than being inside under the sharp eyes of a mean mistress.

Still, she and her family members were often hired out to different farms, and she missed them—her mother most of all. More than once, Minty risked getting a whipping by sneaking out to visit her mother at a nearby plantation. One of Minty's brothers would stand guard outside the cabin door, watching for the slave owner or slave patrols, while Minty visited her mother and sister.

Field hands pick cotton on a Southern plantation in this 1853 engraving. Minty preferred hard field work rather than toiling indoors as a house slave.

This woodcut displays the remarkable meteor shower Minty witnessed on November 12, 1833. Thousands of shooting stars raced across the night sky.

It was on one of those visits, on November 12, 1833, that Minty's brother called her to come outside and see the stars. Thousands of shooting stars lit the night sky. It was a **meteor shower**, and Minty and her family all thought the end of the world had come.

No Place to Lie Down

Minty had been hired out to the worst man in the neighborhood. Instead of paying Brodess for her work, the man agreed to provide Minty with food and clothing, but neither was adequately supplied. One night, Minty and the plantation's cook went to a local store to buy some things for their master. Another slave had left the fields without permission and was tracked to the store by his **overseer**. When the overseer ordered Minty to help him tie down the slave so the overseer could beat him, she refused.

The slave broke free and ran. The overseer grabbed a weight from the store counter and threw it. He might have been aiming for the runaway, but it was Minty who was toppled by the blow. The heavy weight hit her in the forehead.

Years later, Minty vividly remembered the weight coming toward her. She had been wearing a shawl over her head and the

The Bucktown Village Store where Minty was almost killed by a blow to her head while trying to help a runaway slave.

weight "broke my skull and cut a piece of that shawl clean off and drove it into my head. They carried me to the house all bleeding and fainting. I had no bed, no place to lie down on at all, and they lay me on the seat of the loom, and I stayed there all that day and next."

They carried me to the house all bleeding and fainting.

Minty's condition was very serious. But doctors were not called to treat sick slaves, nor were slaves able to rest for long. She was sent back to the fields. "I went to work again and there I worked with the blood and sweat rolling down my face till I couldn't see."

Once again, Minty was called useless and sent back to Brodess. Her parents were afraid she would die. They could do nothing for her but pray. When Brodess realized he would be unable to hire Minty out, he tried to sell her. Luckily for Minty and her family, no one wanted to buy a wounded slave.

Minty had a strong will, and she eventually recovered. But after the injury, she suffered from terrible headaches. She also had sleeping spells—one minute she was awake and talking, and the next she was in a sleep so deep that even a whipping could not wake her. Minty also began to have **visions**, and she believed they were warnings and messages from God.

She dreamed of flying to freedom. Music and loud noises that no one else could hear seemed to fill the air around her. Sometimes the sounds were terrifying. Minty had a recurring vision in which horsemen kidnapped slaves. She could hear the galloping hoofbeats and women screaming as their children were torn from them.

Minty had visions of white men kidnapping slaves and galloping away, separating children from their mothers. This 1834 engraving depicts white men kidnapping a free black man to sell him into slavery.

Minty's Lifelong Head Injury

The blow to Minty's head may have led to an illness called narcolepsy, which causes people to fall asleep for no reason. But some historians believe that Minty developed temporal lobe epilepsy, or TLE, after her head injury. People with TLE have sleeping spells and terrible headaches. Bright lights, colorful visions, and dreamlike trances followed by sleepiness are all symptoms of the condition. Minty experienced those very same symptoms.

For years before her escape, Minty had visions of her flight to freedom. In her dream she flew like a bird over fields, towns, and mountains. At last she would reach a great river. She would try to fly, but it appeared "like I wouldn't have the strength, and just as I was sinkin' down, there would be ladies all drest in white over there, and they would put out their arms and pull me 'cross."

Minty believed her visions foretold the future and relied on them to keep her safe.

Deeply religious all her life, Minty became even more so after she recovered. Her religious beliefs were based on African traditions combined with the Baptist, Catholic, and Methodist practices of the South. Before the slave revolt organized by Nat Turner in nearby Virginia, slaves were allowed to have their own Sunday church services. After the revolt, slaves were allowed to attend only the same church services as their white slave owners. It's possible that Minty and her family were sometimes given

Minty knew many Bible passages by heart. This candle burns on top of a Bible in front of her picture.

permission to attend camp meetings, which were outdoor worship services—with lots of singing and praise—that were led by free black women preachers like Sojourner Truth. Minty knew many Bible passages by heart and turned to them for strength.

Reunited with Ben Ross

Surviving from one day to the next was Minty's biggest challenge. Brodess had tried to sell her several times, but he couldn't find a buyer. Eventually, in 1835 or 1836, she was well enough to be hired out to a master named John T. Stewart, and she lived with him for the next five or six years.

Stewart's plantation had lumbering and ship building businesses, in addition to fields of wheat and corn. Minty's father, Ben Ross, was a highly skilled lumberman, who was often hired out to Mr. Stewart and later managed the shipping of Stewart's timber. At the time Stewart hired Minty, he also employed some of her brothers. Stewart may have been doing Ross a favor by agreeing to take his children, which enabled them to reunite with their father.

Minty grew strong in her years working for Stewart. She lifted huge barrels loaded with goods bound for the market and

Nat Turner's Rebellion

Nat Turner was a popular religious leader to his fellow slaves in Southampton County, Virginia. He believed that he had been chosen by God to lead his people to freedom. On August 22, 1831, he and about seven other slaves killed their master and his family. Slaves from nearby plantations joined in the rebellion, but by August 24 the rebellion had been squashed. More than fifty whites were killed during the uprising. No one knows how many slaves died at the hands of the **militia** and white mobs. Turner was hanged after a sensational trial.

Harriet and her family, who lived less than a hundred miles from Nat Turner's plantation, may have felt inspired by Turner and the slaves who fought with him. But frightened slave owners throughout the South put even tighter controls on their slaves' movements. Blacks were no longer allowed to gather for church services or to visit family members. Whites feared that if blacks got together, they would plan another rebellion.

This nineteenth-century engraving shows Nat Turner meeting with his allies, just before their uprising. Slave owners were so frightened by Nat Turner's rebellion that they put strict controls on slave gatherings.

Teams of oxen, like the ones shown in this nineteenth-century engraving, hauled cotton from plantations to rivers for shipment. When oxen were unavailable, Minty had to carry huge barrels on her back.

pulled heavy boats through the **Eastern Shore**'s canal system "like an ox." Eventually, she was put to work in the fields and the woods, where she drove oxen, plowed, hauled logs, and chopped wood. She was a small woman, only five feet tall, but she grew to be stronger than many men. Stewart used to call on Minty to perform feats of strength for his friends, just to show her off.

In 1836, Ben Ross's master, Anthony Thompson, died. In his will, he granted Ben Ross his freedom when he reached the age of forty-five. Thompson also gave him ten acres of land to live on for the rest of his life. Four years after Thompson's death, when his son determined that Ben Ross had reached forty-five, he set Ben free. His wife and children were still slaves, however, so Ben remained in the area and continued to work for the Thompsons and the Stewarts. Only now, he earned wages.

Maryland was one of the few Southern states to have a large community of free blacks—slaves who had been freed by their masters and blacks who had been born free. It became so common for slave owners to grant freedom to slaves when they were too old to work any longer that in order to keep the number of free blacks down, Maryland passed a law that said slaves who were not capable of working or who were over the age of fifty could not be freed.

Marriage to John Tubman

In 1844, Minty was granted permission to marry John Tubman, a free black man. Very little is known about John Tubman, or how the couple met and fell in love. Marriages between free black men and slave women were rare. John must have loved Minty very much, knowing that whatever children they would have would be born slaves. He also knew that his wife could be sold at any time. At some point in history, Minty changed her name to Harriet, and thus, after her marriage to John, she became Mrs. Harriet Tubman.

John must have loved Minty very much, knowing that whatever children they would have would be born slaves.

In Maryland, it wasn't unusual for trusted slaves like Harriet to get permission to hire themselves out to other slave owners, as long as the slaves paid their masters. Harriet had such an arrangement with Edward Brodess. As long as she paid Brodess fifty to sixty dollars a year, she was allowed to keep the rest of her wages.

Minty and John Tubman were probably married by a black preacher, like the couple shown in this slave marriage ceremony. Slaves were married on Sundays, their only day off.

What's in a Name?

Araminta, or Minty, may have changed her name to Harriet to celebrate the fact that she lived after recovering from that terrible blow to her head. Some historians believe that she changed her name when she married John Tubman. Yet others think that she adopted her new name when she gained her freedom from slavery. We may never know exactly when or why Minty changed her name, but historians do agree that she took the name Harriet to honor the mother she loved so much.

For the first five years of her marriage, Harriet remained legally a slave but lived on other plantations and hired herself out to John Stewart and later to Dr. Anthony C. Thompson, the son of Anthony Thompson, Ben Ross's former owner. Harriet worked so hard plowing fields and hauling timber, that she had earned forty dollars, enough to buy a team of oxen. She could then hire herself out for even higher wages. She and John probably hoped to save enough money to buy Harriet's freedom.

But Edward Brodess had other plans. He was struggling financially and wanted to sell Harriet right away. He needed more money than the fifty to sixty dollars she paid him every year. Harriet prayed that God would change her master's heart.

"I prayed all night long for master, till the first of March; and all the time he was bringing people to look at me, and trying to sell me. Then we heard that some of us was going to be sold to go with the chain-gang down to the cotton and rice fields, and they said I was going, and my brothers, and sisters. Then I changed my prayer. First of March I began to pray, 'Oh Lord if you ain't never going to change that man's heart, kill him, Lord, and take him out of the way.'"

To the Highest Bidder

Harriet didn't know that as she prayed, Edward Brodess was dying. On March 7, 1849, he passed away. Harriet was shocked, and she worried that her prayers had killed him. "Next thing I heard old master was dead, and he died just as he lived," Harriet said. "Oh, then, it appeared like I'd give all the world full of gold, if I had it, to bring that poor soul back. But I couldn't pray for him no longer." His death did not spare Harriet from being sold, as she had feared. Brodess's widow asked the court to allow her to sell some of her husband's slaves to pay his debts.

On June 27, Eliza Brodess posted an advertisement to sell Harriet's niece, also named Harriet. The twenty-year-old was one of the daughters that Linah had been forced to leave behind so many years before. The auction never took place, but on August 29, Eliza Brodess offered to sell Linah's other daughter, Kessiah, to the highest bidder.

The entire family lived in terror of being sold. Harriet realized that in order to prevent this from happening, and avoid being taken from her husband and the rest of her family forever, she would have to run away.

TO BE SOLD,

A Likely negro Man, his Wife and Child ; the negro Man capable of doing all forts of Plantation Work, and a good Miller : The Woman exceeding fit for a Farmer, being capable of doing any Work, belonging to a Houfe in the Country, at reafonable Rates, inquire of the Printer hereof.

This newspaper advertisement offers slaves for sale "at reasonable rates," including a man, his wife, and their child.

CHAPTER 3

Liberty or Death

There was one of two things I had a right to, liberty or death; if I could not have one, I would have the other.

Harriet tried to convince John Tubman to run away with her, but he refused. Later, Harriet would never talk about his reasons for this. As a free man, John could leave Maryland at any time, but he wouldn't leave with her. Perhaps he was afraid of leaving the only home he had ever known.

But Harriet was determined to be free, with or without her husband. "I had reasoned this out in my mind," she said many years later. "There was one of two things I had a right to, liberty or death; if I could not have one, I would have the other."

Harriet was working for Dr. Anthony C. Thompson at the time, and possibly her brothers Ben and Henry were also hired out to the same slave owner. This allowed them to escape together. It is unknown if they planned their escape for weeks or days ahead, or if they set out on the spur of the moment. Harriet kept it a secret even from her husband, and on September 17, 1849, she and her brothers crept into the night and made a dash for freedom.

About two weeks later, on October 3, an advertisement for their capture was published in the newspaper. Eliza Brodess offered a reward for the three runaways—fifty dollars each if they were taken in the state of Maryland, and one hundred dollars each if they were found outside the state. In the newspaper advertisement, Harriet was described as, "MINTY, aged about 27 years, is of a chestnut color, fine looking, and about 5 feet high."

However, by the time the ad was published, the three had already turned back. Ben and Henry had disagreed with Harriet about directions and grew too afraid to continue. Harriet begged them to keep going, but they were more afraid of what would happen to them if they were captured than if they returned to Eliza Brodess voluntarily. They turned back, and dragged an angry and disappointed Harriet with them.

THREE HUNDRED DOLLARS REWARD.

RANAWAY from the subscriber on Monday the 17th ult., three negroes, named as follows: HARRY, aged about 19 years, has on one side of his neck a wen, just under the ear, he is of a dark chestnut color, about 5 feet 8 or 9 inches hight ; BEN, aged aged about 25 years, is very quick to speak when spoken to, he is of a chestnut color, about six feet high ; MINTY, aged about 27 years, is of a chestnut color, fine looking, and about 5 feet high. One hundred dollars reward will be given for each of the above named negroes, if taken out of the State, and $50 each if taken in the State. They must be lodged in Baltimore, Easton or Cambridge Jail, in Maryland.

ELIZA ANN BRODESS.

Near Bucktown, Dorchester county, Md.
Oct. 3d, 1849.

☞The Delaware Gazette will please copy the above three weeks, and charge this office.

Shown here is Eliza Brodess's advertisement offering a reward of $100 each for Minty and two of her brothers after their first escape attempt.

There is no record of the punishment she and her brothers must have received when they returned home, but their mother, Rit, would have likely been overjoyed to see them again. Rit's happiness over getting her daughter back would be short-lived, since Harriet was determined to try again.

Bound for the Promised Land

Dorchester County and the rest of Maryland's Eastern Shore was crisscrossed by dozens of rivers, creeks, and marshes. These waterways made it possible for slaves and their owners to move around easily, and for free blacks to carry messages from one community to the next. No doubt some of those messages, passed from boatman to boatman, free black to slave, carried rumors of a secret network of people that would help a slave escape to the North. Harriet was about to discover this network.

Shortly after returning home, Harriet stole away again. This time she went alone.

Shortly after returning home, Harriet stole away again. This time she went alone. She couldn't tell anyone about her plans, especially her mother. Rit had already lost too many children, and Harriet was afraid her mother's tears and moans would give her away. But she couldn't leave without saying good-bye.

On the night she escaped, Harriet offered to do her mother's chores so Rit could rest. Then she went to the big house to confide in a slave named Mary. Just as Harriet was about to share her secret with Mary, Dr. Thompson rode up on horseback and surprised them. Slaves rarely spoke or sang when Thompson was around, but Harriet was desperate to leave a message, so she sang a hymn in a rich clear voice as she casually walked away.

I'm sorry I'm going to leave you
Farewell, oh farewell;
But I'll meet you in the morning,
Farewell, oh farewell.

I'll meet you in the morning,
I'm bound for the Promised Land,
On the other side of Jordan,
Bound for the Promised Land.

Harriet went back to the big house again a little while later, hoping to confide in Mary, but Thompson was still in the yard. So Harriet sang louder. Then she fled into the night. Her song would have to serve as her good-bye.

Traveling alone and using the **North Star** to guide her, Harriet headed for Pennsylvania. The details of her escape and the names of the people who helped her along the way were so secret that they are still unknown today. We do know, however, that she was aided by both whites and blacks.

Harriet's first helper was a white woman who lived nearby. She was probably a Quaker woman who knew Harriet. The Quakers, a Christian group that spoke out against slavery, were some of the most important members of the Underground Railroad, a network of black and white people who helped

A nineteenth-century engraving of a Quaker meeting in Philadelphia. The Quakers were antislavery activists and important members of the Underground Railroad.

The Underground Railroad

Slaves had been running away from their **slaveholders** ever since slavery began in North America. At first, many slaves escaped to Spanish-controlled Florida, or into the western territories. Some joined Native American tribes. As the country expanded, and slavery was abolished in the North, slaves ran to these Free States. Secret networks of whites and free blacks helped the **fugitives** on their way to freedom.

In the 1830s, these secret networks became more organized and took on the name Underground Railroad. It was neither underground nor a railroad. Legend has it that the name came about when a slave owner from Kentucky claimed

Underground Railroad conductors help a family of escaping slaves in this 1893 painting by Charles T. Webber.

that the runaway slave he was chasing must have escaped using an underground road after he seemed to disappear.

Members of the Underground Railroad saw themselves as a secret army, fighting a nonviolent war against slavery. The complicated network stretched from the South all the way to Canada.

This secret army adopted the terminology of the railroads that were rapidly spreading across the United States at the time. Guides, known as conductors, led fugitive slaves, known as cargo or passengers, from one safe hiding place to the next. **Safe houses** were often called stations or depots, and the Underground Railroad volunteers who ran them were known as stationmasters.

The work of the Underground Railroad was so secret that very few records survive—almost nothing was written down. Penalties for white conductors were harsh—including steep fines and long prison sentences. Black conductors suffered even more when they were caught, and they could have been put to death, especially in the South. Their jobs were so dangerous that most people involved in the Underground Railroad only knew the names of one or two others. Despite the constant danger, thousands of people secretly helped fugitive slaves make their way from one station to the next, because they believed that everyone should live free.

smuggle slaves to freedom. Harriet gave the woman a prized quilt she had made herself and carried with her. Whether it was a thank-you gift or a payment for the woman's help is unknown, but the white woman told Harriet the names of the next two people who would help her on her journey, and gave her a piece of paper with their names. Harriet, of course, could not read what was written on the paper she carried, but she could offer it as proof to the person named on it that she was a runaway slave. Harriet had begun her long ride on the Underground Railroad.

Harriet traveled at night and mostly on foot, from Maryland to Delaware and on to Pennsylvania.

When Harriet reached the first secret location where fleeing slaves were hidden, a white woman asked her to sweep the front yard. Harriet must have been confused, but she soon realized that sweeping would make her look like an obedient slave to anyone who passed by. When it got dark, Harriet was told to lie down in a wagon. The woman's husband covered her with goods so she could not be seen and took her to the next house.

Harriet's escape might not have been noticed for a few days. Her masters were used to the fact that she hired herself out to various employers. But eventually her disappearance would have been discovered, and **handbills** and newspaper advertisements offering a reward for her capture would have put slave catchers on her trail.

Harriet traveled at night and mostly on foot, from Maryland to Delaware and on to Pennsylvania. Delaware was a free state, but it was also the home of many slave catchers. Harriet would not be completely safe until she entered Pennsylvania. She had learned that Pennsylvania was the place

Slave Patrols and Slave Catchers

Most communities in the South had slave patrols—called paddy rollers by the slaves. These patrols were in charge of watching the movements of slaves and punishing those who broke the rules. Any slave found off the plantation without a white person had to have proof that he or she was not a runaway. This proof was usually a written pass, signed and dated by an owner. One of the reasons slaves were not taught to read and write was so that they could not forge their own passes.

As more and more slaves tried to escape, a group of professional bounty hunters, or slave catchers, began to roam the countryside and cities in search of runaway slaves. They were armed with guns, knives, and whips and used vicious dogs to hunt for fugitives. Slave catchers in search of big rewards didn't make sure the person they caught was indeed a slave. Many free blacks were captured by slave catchers and sold into slavery.

Armed slave hunters chase a runaway in this nineteenth-century engraving. Slave catchers roamed the countryside in search of slaves, hoping to claim the rewards offered for their return.

Like this c. 1863 print of an escaping slave, Harriet Tubman hid in swamps and prayed that she wouldn't be discovered.

to go, the same way she had learned about the Underground Railroad—through information secretly passed from free blacks to slaves, and whispered from slave to slave. No doubt, Harriet's Underground Railroad helpers also gave her advice along the way.

Many slaves did not have shoes, and it's not clear if Harriet had to make the long trip barefoot. She made her way through forests and swamps, and ate when she could. Her path was a treacherous one into the unknown, and she must have been afraid. She never knew when a sleeping spell or a terrible headache would come over her. The area would have been filled with armed patrols, and she would've heard the bloodhounds' baying, as she crept from one safe place to the next.

Free at Last

Finally, after a journey that may have taken as long as three weeks, Harriet Tubman crossed the Pennsylvania border. She was free. "When I found I had crossed that line," Harriet later remembered, "I looked at my hands to see if I was the same person. There was such a glory over everything; the sun came like gold through the trees, and over the fields, and I felt like I was in Heaven."

Harriet made her way to Philadelphia. The city, then the fourth largest city in the world, must have seemed magical to the woman from the rural South. Although most blacks lived in one of two poor neighborhoods, Harriet was able to freely wander the sidewalks, and even enjoy public gardens. Black children attended their own public schools. There were black-owned businesses and scores of African American churches. Charities were established to help fugitive slaves.

Philadelphia was the world's fourth largest city when Harriet arrived in 1849. This woodcut shows the city as it was around 1800.

It was probably one of those charities that helped Harriet find a place to sleep and a way to earn money. It's not clear what kind of job Harriet did when she first arrived, but she was young and strong. There was plenty of work for maids and cooks in Philadelphia's many hotels and even in private homes. Harriet quickly blended into the community of free blacks and former slaves, making her own living.

As exciting as her new opportunities must have been, Harriet still wasn't completely free. Under United States law, slaveholders had the power to cross state lines and reclaim their human "property" from Northern towns. Free blacks and slaves alike had to be on a constant lookout for slave catchers. Harriet also worried about the family she had left behind, and no doubt sent a secret message back to them using the Underground Railroad grapevine.

Freedom in Philadelphia did not guarantee happiness. Harriet was lonely. "There was no one to welcome me to the land of freedom," she later said. "I was a stranger in a strange land; and my home, after all, was down in Maryland; because my father, my mother, my brothers, my sisters, and friends were there. But I was free and *they* should be free."

Forced into Action

It's not clear when Harriet decided she would become a conductor on the Underground Railroad. She loved her family, and she missed them, and she wanted them to have the same freedoms she did. Many former slaves shared her views about freedom, but most of them were afraid to help their friends and family. Harriet had the courage to take action. Through the Underground Railroad and free-black sources, she kept in touch with what was going on back home, and she planned for the day when she could liberate her family.

In the summer months, Harriet worked in seaside restaurants like this one, in Cape May, New Jersey, to earn enough money to bring her loved ones north.

In the summer months Harriet left Philadelphia for Cape May, New Jersey, where she could earn more money as a cook and a maid in the oceanfront hotels. Harriet worked hard and saved her money so she could return to Maryland and lead her loved ones north.

It would not be long before she was forced into action to save a member of her family from the auction block. In December 1850, Harriet learned from friends in Baltimore that her niece Kessiah, known as Kizzy, was for sale again. John Bowley, Kizzy's free black husband, turned to Harriet for help. She was the one person he knew who had successfully escaped to the North, and she may have already let her family know that she would do what she could to liberate them.

If Harriet was going to keep Kizzy and her two children from being auctioned off, she had to act fast.

CHAPTER 4

Daring Rescues

My home, after all, was down in Maryland; because my father, my mother, my brothers, my sisters, and friends were there. But I was free and they should be free.

It took extraordinary courage for Harriet to travel back to a slave state to rescue her niece Kizzy. If Harriet was caught, she would surely be forced into slavery again. Eliza Brodess could sell her in a state like Alabama, Mississippi, Louisiana, or Georgia, where most of the country's cotton and rice plantations were located. The **Deep South** was hotter than Maryland and the work in the fields was even more difficult. Escape from the Deep South was almost impossible, since the slaves were simply too far from the North. Getting captured and sold would also mean that Harriet would never see her family again. And if she were caught trying to rescue another slave, her penalty could have been death. But Harriet, knowing that one of the people she loved needed her, put her fears aside and traveled to Baltimore. She didn't dare go into Dorchester County, where she used to live.

Harriet's brother-in-law, Tom Tubman, kept her hidden in Baltimore while she and John Bowley, Kizzy's free black husband, tried to come up with a plan. Tom Tubman probably worked on Baltimore's docks. He must have known the purpose of Harriet's visit, but whether he played any role in the planning or the rescue is unknown.

Baltimore, shown in this 1856 engraving, had a large community of free blacks and a bustling port, making it a safer place for Harriet than Dorchester County, where she was well known.

It's also unknown if Harriet's husband had any idea about where she was and what she was planning. By the time Kizzy and her two children were taken to the slave trader, Harriet and John Bowley had come up with a daring rescue scheme.

Harriet's First Rescue

On the day of the auction, Kizzy held her infant daughter, Araminta, in her arms. Her six-year-old son James stood beside her on the courthouse steps. Slave sales were like county fairs in the South. People came from all over to watch the action and mingle with the crowd. Kizzy's husband joined the crowd of buyers. In Maryland, there was no law against a man buying his family, so when the bidding started, John Bowley bid for his wife and children as if he had all the money in the world. The price for a healthy young woman and her two children could have been as high as $500 or $600. Finally, the other buyers dropped out.

Whites came from all over to watch the action at slave auctions like this one. Slaves desperately hoped they wouldn't be sold away from their families.

John Bowley had won the auction. That was a lot of money for a free black man to pay. Kizzy and her children wouldn't be handed over to John until he paid up. They were told to wait while the auctioneer went to dinner.

When the auctioneer returned and called for payment, John Bowley didn't come forward. He had disappeared. The auctioneer shrugged and started the bidding again. It wouldn't have been the first time that a buyer who didn't really have the money got caught up in a bidding war. But then someone whispered something in his ear and the bidding was stopped. Kizzy and her children had disappeared, too.

Kizzy's master searched the town for her, but she could not be found. Walking through the large crowd that had gathered for the auction, John Bowley had managed to sneak his family into the home of a white woman who lived just five minutes from the courthouse. That night, under cover of darkness, John secretly took his wife and children on a small boat and sailed for Baltimore, seventy-five miles away. It was a dangerous journey in rough December waters. It would have taken at least a full day of sailing—maybe even longer, in bad weather. It's possible that they found shelter along the way in free black communities on the waterfront. The family made it safely to Baltimore, where Harriet hid them among her friends for a few days before leading Kizzy and her children from station to station on the Underground Railroad. When the family reached safety in Philadelphia, Kizzy took a new name to celebrate her new freedom. She became Mary Anne.

It was a dangerous journey in rough December waters.

Harriet had made her first rescue. But it wasn't enough. She still had many family members trapped in slavery, and she wasn't about to rest until all the people she loved were together and free in the North.

A few months later, in the spring of 1851, she went back to Baltimore to lead her brother Moses and two other men to freedom. It was her second successful journey. Like most of Harriet's rescues, the details were kept secret, but Harriet tried to keep far away from Dorchester County, where she could be easily recognized, even though it was the place where most of her loved ones lived.

Slave Marriages

Marriages between slaves, or slaves and free blacks, were not legal. The commitments made between African Americans were informal ones that slave owners could choose to honor or ignore. Sometimes masters forced their slaves into marriages to produce slave children, or sold one member of a couple when they disapproved of a match.

Most slaves married for love and fought against the control of their masters. Weddings were always held on Sundays, the slaves' only day off. Preachers sometimes spoke at the ceremony, but most newlyweds took part in an African custom called jumping the broom. The bride and groom would each jump backward over a broom handle held a few inches above the floor.

Slaves had to live with the knowledge that their masters could break up their marriage at any time.

A couple gets ready to jump the broom in this slave marriage ceremony. Jumping the broom was an African custom.

Betrayal

In fall 1851, Harriet took her biggest gamble up until that time. Even though John Tubman had refused to go to Pennsylvania with her two years earlier, Harriet still loved him and hoped they could be together. She returned to her former home to bring her husband north. She saved up her earnings, bought him a new suit, and traveled back home. Her route and whether she traveled by boat or on foot are still unknown.

When Harriet arrived, she discovered that John had taken a new wife. Harriet hid with friends nearby and sent word to John that she was waiting for him. He refused to join her. He had a free wife and would not be leaving his home for Harriet. Harriet was shocked and sad. She had risked her freedom so that they could be together, and John turned her down. He wouldn't even go see her. Her dream of a free life with her husband was over. She decided to "go right in and make all the trouble she could." But she soon realized that would simply lead to her capture. If John Tubman could live without her, she decided she could live without him: "he dropped out of [my] heart," Harriet later said.

But she had more than heartbreak to worry about. Dorchester County was a dangerous place for her. Slave patrols and her former masters would recognize her instantly. She must have wondered if John Tubman or someone else would betray her to earn a reward.

New Dreams

When Harriet learned that her husband had married another woman, her outlook on life changed. Her dreams for the future were shattered, and she had to come up with new ones. Harriet made a firm commitment to the work of the Underground

Railroad—not just for her own family, but for any slave who wanted to be free. Harriet let go of her anger and her sadness, and she gathered together a group of slaves and led them to Philadelphia. No doubt, she gave one of those slaves the suit she had bought for her husband.

Harriet may have made another trip back to Dorchester County a couple of months later to bring out a group of eleven slaves, including another brother and his wife. It's very likely that this group of fugitives stayed at the home of Frederick Douglass, the most prominent African American leader of the day, in Rochester, New York.

Frederick Douglass (1818–1895)

Frederick Douglass was one of the most famous and respected African American journalists and antislavery leaders during Harriet Tubman's years with the Underground Railroad. Douglass himself was an escaped slave who later bought his freedom. Born in Talbot County, Maryland, he secretly used his master's son's books to teach himself to read. He escaped from Baltimore as a young man, and later published his autobiography, *Life and Times of Frederick Douglass*. Douglass and Tubman used the same Underground Railroad networks to escape and help others to freedom.

Frederick Douglass, shown in this undated photograph, helped slaves fleeing to freedom.

The passage of the Fugitive Slave Act in September 1850—nicknamed the Bloodhound Law after the dogs that were used to track down fugitive slaves—meant that slave catchers had even more power than before. Fugitives and even free blacks could be seized at any time, dragged before a judge, and sent back to slavery—simply on the word of one white slave owner or slave catcher. Blacks, free or fugitive, were powerless to speak on their own behalf. To make sure that her family and friends were safe, Harriet now had to lead her passengers even farther north. "I wouldn't trust Uncle Sam with my people no longer, but I brought 'em clear to Canada," Harriet said.

This hand-colored woodcut depicts an escaped slave who is captured under the Fugitive Slave Act. Escaped slaves were in constant danger of being arrested and sent back to the South.

Fugitive Slave Act

Southern slaveholders always had the legal right to recover escaped slave "property" from the North, but many Free States refused to return fugitive slaves to their owners.

Southern slaveholders grew more and more angry over the high number of runaway slaves. When Congress moved to admit two new Free States—California and New Mexico—to the Union, there were two more Free States than slave states. Southern congressmen demanded that the federal government give them some protection. Congress tried to avoid a civil war by passing the Fugitive Slave Act in September 1850. The **abolitionists** nicknamed it the Bloodhound Law.

The law gave slave catchers the power to force local authorities, like the police and judges, to help slave masters capture their human "property." Anyone caught helping runaway slaves had to pay heavy fines and could be sent to jail. Anyone suspected of being a runaway could be arrested and turned over to slave catchers. The government paid judges ten dollars for every black they sent back to slavery, but only five dollars if they ruled that a black person was indeed free.

Northerners were outraged, especially because the law gave slave catchers the authority to insist that onlookers help them capture alleged fugitives. One newspaper, the Ohio *Standard*, wrote, "Now we are all slave catchers." Free blacks and fugitives were no longer safe in the North.

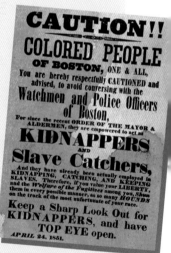

A handbill warns Boston African Americans to be on the lookout for kidnappers and slave catchers after the passage of the Fugitive Slave Act of 1850.

CHAPTER 5

The Moses of Her People

Oh go down, Moses, Way down into Egypt's land.

Harriet Tubman settled her group in St. Catharines, Ontario, where other fugitives from Dorchester County had established themselves, and stayed there for several months. The first winter was very hard. They were either given a house, or they built their own. The group had little food and no warm clothing for the cold winter months. Harriet chopped wood and kept house. With the help of local charities they made it through the first winter. In the spring she went back to Philadelphia to earn enough money to bring more slaves to freedom.

Her successful trip with eleven slaves made her consider larger and larger rescues. But Harriet was afraid she wasn't strong enough or brave enough to fulfill her new mission. Later she remembered: "The Lord

Harriet's family, like other Dorchester County fugitives, settled safely in St. Catharines, Ontario, which can be seen just across the border from New York State.

told me to do this. I said, 'Oh, Lord, I can't—don't ask me—take somebody else.'" But Harriet believed that God answered: "It's you I want, Harriet Tubman."

Her mission would lead her to be called the Moses of her people. Like the Moses in the Bible who led the Jews out of Egypt, Harriet Tubman would lead her people out of slavery, and she would go on to become the most famous conductor on the Underground Railroad.

Harriet's Escape Tricks

In 1852, Harriet began making one trip a year, and sometimes two, into slave territory. By the winter of 1853–54, she had made at least five trips and brought thirty slaves to freedom. We don't know exactly how Harriet got word to runaways, or how the slaves were chosen and gathered for these trips north.

Although Harriet kept no record of her raids, we do know that she stayed on back roads and traveled by night. When the skies were cloudy and she could not see the North Star, Harriet would feel the moss on tree trunks. Since she knew that moss grew only on the north side of tree trunks, she could tell which way was north. The long dark nights of late fall and early winter were her favorite times to travel. She collected her passengers far from their homes and often met them in cemeteries, where groups of pretend mourners might go unnoticed.

Slaves were often not missed on Sundays, their one day off, and newspapers with runaway-slave advertisements were not printed on Sundays, so Harriet would leave on Saturday nights to get the biggest possible head start before the slaveholders discovered their slaves were missing. She also paid free blacks to follow behind white masters as they posted reward notices for runaways and tear them down.

When shuttling people along the Underground Railroad on rainy nights when she couldn't see the North Star, Harriet used moss to find her way north. Harriet knew that moss grew only on the north side of tree trunks, as in the above photograph.

Harriet guided her groups by singing spirituals and songs with coded messages. When danger was nearby, she would warn them with: "Oh, go down, Moses/ Way down into Egypt's land." But when the road was clear, she would sing: "Hail, oh hail, ye happy spirits/ Death no more shall make you fear."

Hardships and Close Calls

Angry masters could appear at any time, along with armed patrols and bloodhounds. The long trip on foot was especially difficult on the children, since most of them had no shoes. They may have left bloody footprints on icy winter paths, and walking in the rain and snow, the slaves' skin would chafe against their coarse clothing and bleed. Every step toward freedom was a painful one.

The long trip on foot was especially difficult on the children, since most of them had no shoes.

Freedom Songs

Music was important in slave communities. They developed their own songs, called spirituals, based on Christian hymns. These songs made the workday go faster, and they could also contain hidden messages.

A slave humming "Go Down Moses" might be passing the word that Harriet Tubman was near. "Wade in the Water" was sung to warn escaped slaves that bloodhounds were on their trail and they needed to get into the water to throw the dogs off their scent.

One legendary Underground Railroad conductor, a one-legged sailor named Peg Leg Joe, taught slaves to sing "Follow the Drinking Gourd." Hidden in the lyrics were directions for following the Underground Railroad to the Ohio River, where slaves could cross from Kentucky into Ohio, a Free State. The "drinking gourd" was the Big Dipper, a constellation of stars that pointed to the North Star, and to freedom.

Slaves sang spirituals with hidden meanings at gatherings like this corn husking.

Babies were given opium, a drug that made them sleep, so they wouldn't cry and give the fugitives away on their treks through swamps and forests. Tubman also carried a gun. Her goal was to protect herself and the groups. No one was allowed to lose heart and turn back. Harriet was forced to threaten scared slaves who wanted to go home, since she knew that a dead fugitive could not tell on those who had helped him or her or what secret route they had taken, but she never had to shoot. And unlike most conductors on the Underground Railroad, Tubman never lost a passenger.

Harriet had friends up and down her many routes, helping her along the way. She knew which Quaker meetinghouse had a secret loft, and who had a hidden room above his kitchen. Once,

Sliding shelves in the Gettysburg, Pennsylvania, home of Reverend Alexander Dobbin were built to hide runaway slaves in a crawl space.

she and three soaked passengers took refuge with a free black family after crossing two rivers. The punishment for helping runaways was severe, but the black family allowed the fugitives to dry off and sleep during the dangerous daylight hours. Harriet had no money to pay the family, and she knew that they were desperately poor. She wanted to thank them for risking their lives to help her and her passengers, so she gave them the only thing she could spare— her undergarments.

Harriet became an expert actress and often disguised herself as an old woman or an old man. During one difficult rescue of a large group, she found herself face-to-face with a group of Irish workers on a bridge, probably in Delaware. Harriet strolled up and began a casual conversation. Because she wasn't hiding, or acting afraid, the workers were not suspicious and assumed that Harriet and her passengers were free blacks. The group walked over the bridge, talking and laughing as if nothing were wrong.

Like this nineteenth-century engraving of a fugitive female slave disguised as a man, Tubman often dressed herself up as a man or an old woman in order to pass through dangerous territory.

"When danger is near, it appears like my heart goes flutter, flutter," Harriet later said. Many fugitives reported that she would insist that they stop for no reason, and then start out in a new direction. Only later did they discover that slave catchers had been lying in wait for them. Harriet relied on her **intuition** to keep herself and her passengers safe.

Harriet relied on her intuition to keep herself and her passengers safe.

Her physical strength and ability to carry on while in terrible pain were important traits of the woman called Moses. On one northbound trip, she had a terrible toothache. The infection got worse and worse, but rather than stop and get help, Harriet knocked out her own tooth with her pistol and ended her pain.

Throughout this time, Harriet continued to have terrible headaches and sleeping spells. The slaves in her care must have been terrified that she would fall asleep at the wrong moment. She was the one person who knew where the next Underground Railroad station was located and who could lead them to safety. But Harriet never let them down.

She was the one person who knew where the next Underground Railroad station was located . . .

She often took on rescue assignments to bring the relatives of other fugitives north. She made many quick raids into Maryland and Virginia to rescue slaves who were about to be sold to the Deep South. She slipped the slaves over the Pennsylvania border, into the hands of other Underground Railroad conductors, and headed back for more.

Once, Harriet took on the job of finding the sweetheart of an escaped slave and stole the young woman, named Tilly, from her master in Maryland. Tilly's fiancé had been waiting for her for eight years. Harriet used a forged certificate, which stated that she was a free woman, and found a steamboat captain in Delaware willing to issue a travel permit for Tilly. When resting for a night in a hotel, a slave dealer found them there and tried to capture them. But the hotelkeeper, who was sympathetic to Harriet and Tilly's plight, held him up while the two women made a fast getaway. Somehow, Harriet managed to buy railroad tickets to Camden, Delaware, and from there, they traveled to Philadelphia, where Tilly was reunited with her sweetheart— probably in the office of William Still, an underground operator and leader in the fight against slavery.

Dinah Morris, a freed slave, shows her papers to prove she is not a slave. Harriet sometimes secured forged papers for her "passengers" so they could travel safely.

While Tilly and her fiancé made their way to Canada, Harriet went back to Maryland, where she rescued a woman and three children. Tubman had many successes, but she failed on two trips between 1852 and 1854 to bring the rest of her family north. She could not rest until her entire family was free.

William Still (1821–1902)

William Still, a Philadelphia Underground Railroad operator, helped hundreds of slaves on their way to freedom. Still's father purchased his own freedom, and his mother escaped from slavery with two of her then four children; she had fourteen more after her escape. William, her youngest child, worked at the Pennsylvania Society for the Abolition of Slavery. He helped hundreds of newly escaped fugitives, including Harriet Tubman, settle in the North or make their way to Canada. One of the former slaves he helped turned out to be his own brother, one of the two children his mother was forced to leave behind. Still was one of the few Underground Railroad stationmasters to keep careful records of the fugitives who passed through his office on their way to Canada.

He had this to say about Harriet Tubman: "In point of courage, shrewdness and disinterested exertions to rescue her fellow-men, by making personal visits to Maryland among the slaves, she was without her equal."

William Still was a black abolitionist who was an Underground Railroad conductor like Harriet.

CHAPTER 6

Rescuing Family Members

Read my letter to the old folks, and give my love to them.

Between 1851 and 1854, Tubman's brothers Ben, Robert, and Henry Ross tried to run away several times, but each time they were caught and forced to turn back. Harriet tried at least once to bring them out of slavery but failed.

After Edward Brodess's death, a grandson of Atthow Pattison, Rit's original owner, filed a **lawsuit** against Eliza Brodess. Pattison claimed that he was the lawful owner of Rit and her children. This lawsuit was the only thing that kept Eliza Brodess from selling the brothers into the Deep South.

Harriet continued to work as a maid and a cook and to save her money, making important Underground Railroad connections and plotting to free her brothers. She led others to freedom and instructed many more who made their own trips on the Underground Railroad, but she could not help her brothers, who were being closely watched.

During the 1850s, Harriet became friends with a group of well-known abolitionists in the North and was a speaker at more than one antislavery rally. Her appearances were always a last-minute surprise, so as not to alert slave catchers to her whereabouts. Those who heard her described her as a great speaker. Audiences were

Harriet was often a surprise speaker at antislavery meetings like this one, shown in 1841. Audiences were moved by her descriptions of slave life and spellbound by tales of her dangerous escapes.

left breathless as Harriet told of her life as a slave and of her dangerous work for the Underground Railroad. And she would call on her new friends to donate funds for her trips south and for the escaped fugitives who arrived with nothing more than the clothes on their backs and a wish to be free.

With the financial help of these backers, Harriet made another trip to Maryland in December 1854 to rescue her brothers. Since Eliza Brodess planned to sell them right after Christmas, there was no time to lose.

Be Ready to Step Aboard

Harriet asked a friend who could write to send a letter to Jacob Jackson, a free black in Dorchester County. Jacob was suspected of helping runaway slaves, and he knew that his mail would be opened and read before it was delivered. So he and Harriet likely worked out a code ahead of time to use in a letter.

The letter was signed "William Henry Jackson," the name of Jacob's adopted son, and it asked Jacob to "read my letter to the old folks, and give my love to them, and tell my brothers to be always watching unto prayer, and when the good old ship of Zion comes along, to be ready to step aboard."

The postal authorities could not imagine what the letter meant. William Henry had no "old folks" or any brothers, so when Jacob was called to the post office to explain, he threw the letter down and said that it didn't make any sense to him. But he secretly knew who wrote it, and it did make sense. He got word to Harriet's brothers to get ready. She was coming for them.

Harriet had traveled back to Dorchester County many times, knowing that any mistake could lead to her capture. She knew Maryland's swamps, waterways, and back roads well. No doubt she varied her hiding places, staying in swamps, in hideouts in the woods, and with different friends. Luckily, she was never betrayed by any of the trusted black and white helpers that she relied on.

This time Harriet arrived on Christmas Eve, 1854. It was Saturday—the best time to escape—and Eliza Brodess had given permission to let her slaves visit their family members on Christmas Day. She had also posted notices advertising the sale of Robert, Ben, and Henry for Monday. Harriet's father, Ben, had purchased his wife, Rit, from Eliza Brodess for twenty dollars, and the couple lived together in Poplar Neck. The brothers were told to meet after dark and start for their parents' cabin, forty miles away. At that time, Harriet didn't know that Robert's wife, Mary, was ready to give birth to a baby. Robert couldn't tell Mary about his plans, but she must have guessed, because she wouldn't let him leave until after their baby girl was born. Robert finally got away, leaving his wife and three young children behind. It must have been a difficult decision, but it was either flee or be sold.

Harriet often hid in Dorchester Country's swamps and waterways. The slaves in this woodcut escaped to the North through swampland.

Harriet peeked at her mother through the cracks of a corncrib like this one on December 25, 1854. She hadn't seen her mother in five years.

Hiding in a Corncrib

In the meantime, Harriet couldn't wait for Robert. She set out for Poplar Neck with Ben, Henry, and Ben's fiancée, Jane Kane. Robert raced to Poplar Neck alone, hoping to catch up with them. He found them on Christmas morning, hidden in a bin used to store corn. Two other slaves, John Chase and Peter Jackson, were also with them.

Rit expected her sons to come for Christmas dinner. Harriet had not seen her mother for five years, and kept peeking out at her from the cracks in the walls of the **corncrib**. All day long she watched her mother appear at the cabin door, looking for her sons. Harriet must have wanted to run out and hug her mother, but it was too dangerous. Rit would have been so upset at the thought of losing more children that her wails and moans would have betrayed their hiding place.

Harriet's father knew where they were and he sneaked food to them. He also got them supplies, but was careful not to look directly at them. He knew he would be questioned later, and he wanted to be able to say that he had not "seen" his children. He checked on the group many times over the course of that Christmas Day. By nightfall, they were well fed and well rested.

When it was time to leave, Ben tied a handkerchief over his eyes and walked with the group a few miles up the road. After they said good-bye, Ben waited for a long time before he took the blindfold off and headed back home.

The group traveled to Wilmington, Delaware, where they passed through the home of Thomas Garrett, a Delaware merchant who worked tirelessly for the Underground Railroad. He later wrote in a letter that Harriet and one of the men had worn the shoes right off their feet. He gave them two dollars to buy new ones. He also got a carriage to take them to Pennsylvania.

Harriet must have wanted to run out and hug her mother, but it was too dangerous.

On December 29, 1854, the eight fugitives arrived in Philadelphia and were welcomed by William Still. At some point in the journey, two more slaves had joined Harriet and her group.

Eventually, the group made it to St. Catharines, Ontario, Canada, where the brothers were reunited with their niece Kizzy (now Mary Anne) and the other friends and family who had already settled there. Like others who had safely made it to freedom, Harriet's brothers took on new names. It's not clear why they took on the name of a powerful white Maryland family, but they became John, Henry, and Ben Stewart.

Harriet stayed in St. Catharines for a few months, but her work was not done. Slaveholders were on alert, making rescues even harder to pull off. Still, Harriet made a number of successful raids in 1855 and 1856. She brought the wife and child of William Henry Jackson (Jacob Jackson's adopted son) north, and in November 1856 she passed through Thomas Garrett's home with five fugitives.

With the exception of the sisters who had been sold, Harriet had managed to bring out almost all of her brothers and sisters. Only her younger sister Rachel remained, and she was in danger of being sold. Harriet decided to rescue her before that would happen.

More Dangerous Rescues

Harriet spent three months in Dorchester County in 1855, waiting for a chance to bring Rachel and her two children north. Waiting was always a dangerous time for Harriet. During one close encounter in a village, she saw a former master walking toward her. Harriet was wearing a big sunbonnet and carrying a pair of chickens, so she lowered her head and pulled the string attached to the chicken's legs. The noisy fowls squawked so loudly and made such a fuss that the man noticed the chickens and not Harriet.

Another time she saw a former master on a train. Harriet grabbed a newspaper and pretended to read. The slave owner knew that Harriet Tubman couldn't read, so he ignored the black woman who was "reading" the newspaper. Luckily, Harriet held the newspaper right side up! She would later say, "the Lord save me that time too."

Eventually, Harriet was forced to return to the North without Rachel. Rachel's children had been hired out and separated from her, and she would not leave without them. It took five months for Harriet to earn enough money to make another trip south. They faced the same problem, and Rachel again wouldn't leave.

Once again, Harriet gathered a group of passengers and headed north without her sister. One of the slaves in this group, Joe Bailey, had a high reward posted for his capture. Slave catchers were in hot pursuit, and Harriet and her passengers were forced to move slowly and stay hidden for long periods of time. One time they hid in potato holes, pits dug in the ground to store potatoes, while the slave catchers passed within several feet of them. The usual four-day trip to Wilmington took almost two weeks.

A trusted friend got word to Thomas Garrett that Harriet and her group were just across the river from Wilmington, but the bridges were being watched. Garrett hired black bricklayers, who loaded their wagon with bricks and crossed the bridge in the morning. They made sure to greet the police, sing, and shout hello to passersby. They did the same thing going back in the evening, only this time Harriet and her passengers were hidden in the wagon's secret compartment.

The noisy fowls squawked so loudly and made such a fuss that the man noticed the chickens and not Harriet.

Eventually the group made it to Philadelphia, but as they continued on to New York City and up to Canada, Joe grew more and more frightened on the long train trip. When the train came to the bridge over the Niagara River, which separated New York and Canada, Harriet tried to lead the group in song and told them to look at the great Niagara Falls. Joe could not raise his head or join in, and he never saw Niagara Falls. But when Harriet

Thomas Garrett (1789–1871)

Thomas Garrett's home in Wilmington, Delaware, was one of Harriet's regular Underground Railroad stops. A white Quaker who was deeply opposed to slavery, Garrett was a hardware and iron merchant who used his own money to help more than twenty-five hundred runaways over his forty years with the Underground Railroad.

Garrett did this despite the danger he himself and his family faced. Once he was badly beaten and thrown off a train by a group of white Southerners. In 1848, Garrett and another abolitionist were arrested, tried, and found guilty for helping a family of slaves escape. Both men were bankrupted by the steep fines they were forced to pay, but that didn't stop Garrett. He vowed to continue his work. "Thou has left me without a dollar," Garrett told the judge. "I say to thee and to all in this court room, that if anyone knows a fugitive who wants shelter . . . send him to Thomas Garrett and he will befriend him." Garrett continued his work with the Underground Railroad until the **Emancipation Proclamation** put an end to slavery.

A slave shackle rests on a portrait of Thomas Garrett, a white abolitionist who actively helped thousands of runaway slaves in his Wilmington, Delaware, home.

told him they were in Canada, and they were free, Joe's shouts and singing drew a crowd, and he announced that his next trip would be to heaven. He would stay in his new free home for the rest of his life.

On Christmas 1856, Harriet was supposed to go back to the Eastern Shore and try once again to rescue Rachel. Maybe Harriet didn't have enough money, or maybe she was sick. Whatever the reason, she didn't make the trip south again until the following spring. She went expecting to return with Rachel, but when Harriet learned that her parents were in danger, her plans changed.

CHAPTER 7

Tubman's Most Dangerous Rescue

I've seen de real ting, and I don't want to see it on no stage or in no teater.

In March of 1857, eight slaves from Dorchester County organized an escape following a route that Harriet had given them. Her father, Ben Ross, sheltered eight runaways in his home in early March. Harriet also told them to contact Thomas Otwell, a free black man and an Underground Railroad conductor in Dover, Delaware. But Otwell betrayed the group of runaways to win a $3,000 reward. Instead of guiding them north to the next stop on the railroad, he led them to jail.

The Dover Eight, as they came to be called, had managed to break out of jail and disappear into the night. All of them eventually made their way to freedom. Maryland slave owners were determined to punish anyone who had helped the runaway slaves. One such person who was suspected of involvement with the group was a free black minister. Although investigators could not find any evidence of this, they did find a copy in his house of *Uncle Tom's Cabin*, an antislavery novel by Harriet Beecher Stowe. As a result, the minister was sentenced to ten years in prison. Under Maryland law, it was a crime for African Americans to own a copy of this book.

Rumor spread that the investigators would turn to Ben Ross next. They rightly suspected that Ben Ross's house had been used as a hideout by the Dover Eight. Anthony C. Thompson warned Ben that he might be in danger and suggested he leave the state immediately. Although Ben and Rit were free—Ben having been freed by his owner many years ago, and Rit having had Ben purchase her freedom for twenty dollars—they knew that Ben would surely be arrested if it became known that they were leaving. In June 1857, Harriet went back to the Eastern Shore of Maryland to take her parents and bring them north to safety.

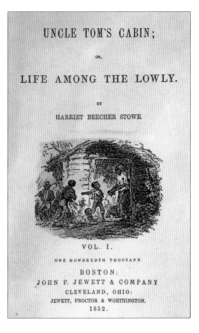

The title page of the 100,000th copy of *Uncle Tom's Cabin* by Harriet Beecher Stowe. The novel sold 300,000 copies in the United States in the first year.

An Escape for Rit and Ben

It took Harriet a long time to make her way south. Slave patrols were everywhere and the short summer nights were dangerous. Harriet knew that her parents, both in their seventies, would not be able to walk all night and try to sleep during the day. She bought an old horse and made a makeshift carriage for them to ride in on the first leg of their journey.

Uncle Tom's Cabin

Harriet Beecher Stowe, the daughter and wife of prominent antislavery ministers, wrote *Uncle Tom's Cabin* in response to the Fugitive Slave Act. The novel, which was based on actual slave stories, brought the horrors of slavery to life.

The stories ran in an antislavery newspaper and were published as a book in March 1852. It immediately captured the public's imagination and became an international sensation. Thousands of ordinary Americans who were previously indifferent to slavery began to condemn it after reading the book. Southern newspapers blasted the book and its author, and efforts were made to ban it, but copies sold anyway.

Although Harriet Tubman could not read the book, she turned down a chance to see one of the many plays based on the novel. "I haint got no heart to go and see the sufferings of my people played out on de stage," she said. "I've seen de *real ting*, and I don't want to see it on no stage or in no teater."

A decade after the book was published, Abraham Lincoln welcomed Harriet Beecher Stowe to the White House with the famous words, "So you are the little woman who wrote the book that made this great war."

Harriet Beecher Stowe was the author of *Uncle Tom's Cabin*, the first book that described of the horrors of slavery.

Harriet led them for eighty miles to Wilmington, Delaware, on an "old horse, fitted out in primitive style with a straw collar, a pair of old chaise wheels, and a board on the axle to sit on." Rit did not want to leave her feather mattress behind, and Harriet agreed to take it along.

When they reached Wilmington, Thomas Garrett gave them money to travel the rest of the way to Canada by train. They stopped in William Still's office in Philadelphia and were eventually reunited in Canada with their sons, several grandchildren, and new great-grandchildren whom they had never met. Like other fugitives, they changed their names when they reached freedom. They chose the same last name as their sons: Stewart.

Harriet led them for eighty miles to Wilmington, Delaware, on an "old horse, fitted out in . . . a pair of old chaise wheels, and a board on the axle to sit on."

Harriet must have wanted to stay with her family in Canada, but her sister Rachel was still a slave. Harriet went back to Dorchester County before the end of the summer and stayed through the fall, hiding in the homes of free black friends, in slave quarters, or in the swamps and forests she knew so well. Once again, Rachel's children were hired out and she would not leave without them.

Although Rachel refused to come north, Harriet gave instructions to help others escape. A group of thirty-nine slaves from the Eastern Shore made it safely north that fall. Fifteen of them belonged to Samuel Pattison, one of the heirs of Rit's first master. Samuel Pattison woke up one morning to discover that his slaves had left him with no one to work on his farm or make his breakfast. Large numbers of slaves were fleeing Maryland.

Slaveholders became so watchful that it was impossible for Harriet to get Rachel and her children together in one place so they could head north. She returned to Canada without them.

Harriet went back to St. Catharines and turned her energies to supporting her parents and raising funds for new **refugees**. She also built up her Underground Railroad network, making connections with sympathetic white abolitionists and free blacks who would help her. She resolutely prepared for the day when she could return to Maryland.

General Tubman

It was during this time that Harriet met the man who would become one of the most famous abolitionists: John Brown. Frederick Douglass may have been the one to suggest to Brown that he meet with Tubman. Brown traveled to St. Catharines in April 1858 to ask for her help in an armed revolt against slavery. Brown was so impressed by Tubman that he gave her the name "General Tubman." Harriet was equally impressed by Brown and believed that she had seen him in a dream before they met: "I was in a wilderness sort of place, all rocks and bushes, when a big snake raised his head from behind a rock, and while I looked, it changed into

Abolitionist John Brown was so impressed with Tubman, he called her "General Tubman" and asked her to help him lead an armed revolt against slavery.

the head of an old man with a long white beard on his chin, and he looked at me wishful like, just as if he was going to speak to me."

John Brown believed that a small band of men, stationed in the Applachian mountains of Virginia, could defend themselves against government forces. He wanted to seize the U.S. armory at Harpers Ferry and distribute its arms to his volunteers. Once the attack began, he believed that free and enslaved blacks alike would join the cause and defeat slavery forever. But both whites and free blacks were skeptical about Brown's plan, and he had trouble raising the money and the **recruits** he needed to wage his battle. Tubman, however, believed in John Brown, and she agreed to help him. In addition to raising money to support her parents, for her own trips back to Maryland, and for the refugee community in Canada, she began to speak to other abolitionists on behalf of Brown.

The reward for her capture was high—perhaps as high as $12,000. . .

Harriet had to be extremely careful when meeting new people as she traveled throughout New England. Her exploits had become known to slaveholders on the Eastern Shore. The reward for her capture was high—perhaps as high as $12,000— and she never knew when she might be betrayed. At the same time, many white abolitionists wanted to meet the great woman who had rescued so many slaves. For her own safety, Harriet began to carry daguerreotypes, a kind of old-fashioned photograph, of her friends. Harriet showed these pictures to each new person she met. If they could not tell her who was in the pictures, then they clearly did not know her abolitionist friends, and they could not be trusted.

Harriet showed photographs like this one of Frederick Douglass to people who wanted to meet her. If they knew her friends, Harriet believed they could be trusted.

A Home in Auburn

William H. Seward, a prominent antislavery senator from Auburn, New York, may have been pictured in one of those daguerreotypes. It's unknown whether or not Seward gave shelter to runaway slaves himself, but Auburn was an important stop on the Underground Railroad, and Harriet knew many people there. As many as five hundred runaways passed through the area over thirty years.

In the spring of 1859, learning that Harriet's parents were having difficulties with the long Canadian winters, Seward offered to sell her a piece of property in Auburn. He allowed Harriet to make a small down payment and pay him a little money at a time. Ben and Rit were happy to relocate, and some historians believe that Harriet herself came back from Canada as a show of defiance against the 1857 Dred Scott case, in which the Supreme Court ruled that slaves like Harriet as well as free blacks were not legal citizens of the United States. Harriet intended to be a full member of American society regardless.

William H. Seward, a senator from Auburn, New York, was one Harriet's friends and supporters. He later became Abraham Lincoln's secretary of state.

Harriet built a house on the property she received from Seward, but the original house was destroyed by fire. Her rebuilt brick house, shown here, still stands today in Auburn, New York.

Dred Scott Case

Dred Scott, a Missouri slave, lived with his owner in free Louisiana territory and in Illinois, a Free State, for many years. After Scott was brought back to Missouri, he sued his owner for his freedom because of his years living in free territories.

Missouri state courts kept Scott in slavery. His lawyers then sued in federal court, and Scott's case eventually made its way to the U.S. Supreme Court.

The Supreme Court, which had a majority of justices from the South, rejected Scott's claim, saying that blacks—free or slave—were inferior to whites and were not full citizens of the United States. The Court wrote that blacks had "no rights which a white man was bound to respect."

The court's ruling became a huge political issue. The gap between those who fought against slavery and those who supported it became even wider. Civil war began to look more and more likely.

A painting of Dred Scott based on a photograph, c. 1858.

CHAPTER 8

The Best Underground Railroad Conductor

I was the conductor on the Underground Railroad for eight years, and I can say what most conductors can't say—I never ran my train off the track and I never lost a passenger.

Throughout the summer of 1859, General Tubman and John Brown met several times to plan the attack on Harpers Ferry. It was Harriet who suggested the Fourth of July as the best day to attack. Harriet continued to speak to abolitionist groups throughout New England, trying to draw recruits and raise funds for the raid.

Despite Tubman's efforts, Brown did not have the men, the weapons, or the funds needed to stage a July fourth attack. It wasn't until the fall of 1859 that Brown was ready, and when he did not hear from Harriet by the end of September, he made plans to go on without her. It was never determined why Harriet did not join Brown in his raid on Harpers Ferry.

On October 16, 1859, at Harpers Ferry, Virginia (now West Virginia), Brown seized a musket factory and the United States armory and won control of the town with just eighteen men. But Brown's plan seemed to end there. The abolitionists, free blacks, and escaped slaves he expected to rush in to fight by his side didn't arrive. His

This contemporary engraving depicts John Brown and his men seizing the armory at Harpers Ferry. They were later trapped inside by the U.S. marines.

forces were quickly surrounded—first by local militia, then by a company of U.S. marines under the command of Colonel Robert E. Lee. Ten of Brown's men, including two of his sons, were killed in the battle that ensued, and Brown was wounded and forced to surrender.

John Brown (1800–1859)

John Brown was a tanner by trade, with twenty children, who devoted his life to his belief in racial equality. In 1850 he responded to the Fugitive Slave Act by organizing a black self-defense group. He moved to Kansas Territory in 1855 and joined a military band with five of his sons after conflict broke out between antislavery and pro-slavery settlers. When five abolitionists were murdered in that conflict, Brown kidnapped five of his pro-slavery neighbors on May 24, 1856, and brutally killed them in revenge.

After this murder, Brown became famous for his opposition to slavery. People on both sides of the slavery debate felt passionately. Some believed he was crazy. Others admired his radical spirit. The attention and financial support he received led him to plan even greater military measures. Three years later, Brown was captured during his raid on Harpers

Brown's surrender at Harpers Ferry was reported in the October 18, 1859, issue of the *New York Times*.

Ferry and charged with **treason** and murder. Harriet Tubman was moved by his words at his trial: "Now if it is deemed necessary that I should forfeit my life for the furtherance of the ends of justice, and mingle my blood with the blood of millions in this slave country whose rights are disregarded by wicked, cruel, and unjust enactments, I say let it be done."

John Brown was hanged in Charles Town, Virginia, in December 1859. His bravery in the face of death inspired his antislavery supporters.

In this c. 1885 painting of John Brown's last moments, a black woman holds her child up for a farewell kiss.

Inspired by Brown

Harriet was in New York City when the raid failed, and during that time she had a premonition that something was wrong but could not say what it was. She told her hostess that Captain Brown was in trouble, and they would hear bad news soon. The next day, they read about his failed raid in the newspaper.

Northern conservatives tried to convince the South that support for Brown was the work of a noisy minority, but the rift between the North and the South, the abolitionists and the pro-slavery people, only grew wider.

Harriet believed that Brown's death was a sign that the time for change was near and that she would see the liberation of black people in her lifetime.

"When I think how he gave up his life for our people, and how he never flinched, but was so brave in the end; it's clear to me it wasn't mortal man, it was God in him. When I think of all the groans and tears and prayers I've heard on plantations, and remember that God is a prayer-hearing God, I feel that His time is drawing near. He gave me my strength, and He set the North Star in the heavens; He meant for me to be free."

Harriet had always thought of slavery as a sin, but Brown's example and his death led her to see that slavery was more than that; it was a state of war—a war she was ready to fight.

In the Thick of It

Inspired by Brown's bravery, she fought to free an escaped slave, Charles Nalle, after he was caught on the streets of Troy, New York. Harriet was just a short distance away when she learned that Nalle had been arrested. Hundreds of antislavery supporters protested outside the office where Nalle was being held. Although she was only about forty years old, Harriet disguised herself as an old woman and slipped into the back of the room. When Nalle was being moved, Harriet signaled the crowd, and she grabbed hold of him.

The sheriff and his deputies started to beat both Harriet and Nalle as the crowd struggled to free them. "Drag us out! Drag him to the river!" Harriet yelled. "Drown him! But don't let them have him." The crowd carried the two of them to the riverfront, where Nalle was rushed into a boat, which took him to West Troy, across the river. Harriet boarded a ferryboat with about three hundred other protesters.

Police officers in West Troy had been alerted and were waiting for Nalle, who was seized and taken to a judge's chambers as soon as his boat landed. Nalle's rescuers stormed the building, but officers guarding the judge's chambers fired on the group. The door to the chambers was then forced open. Harriet rushed past the wounded and grabbed Nalle again. With bullets whizzing past her ears, she threw the fugitive "acrossed my shoulder like a bag o' meal and took him away out of there."

A plaque marks the spot where Charles Nalle was held in Troy, New York, before being rescued by Tubman.

As soon as Nalle had successfully escaped, Harriet slipped back into the crowd. Her clothes were ripped, she was bruised and bloody, but she had won the battle. Harriet had truly become a general.

It may have been this rescue that gave Harriet the courage to make one last attempt to save her sister Rachel. Maryland slaveholders were now even more determined than before to stop the woman known as Moses.

One Final Rescue

Harriet reached the Eastern Shore in late November of 1860, only to learn that Rachel had died months before. Waiting for the right moment to go and search for Rachel's children was too dangerous, so Harriet decided to leave. After ten years of trying

Tubman's Most Puzzling "Rescue"

Late in her career as an Underground Railroad conductor, Harriet made a quick trip south and brought an eight-year-old black girl, Margaret Stewart, back to New York by steamboat. Margaret was placed in the care of William Seward's wife and received special treatment within the family. Whenever Harriet was in town, Margaret would be dressed up and sent in the Seward carriage to visit her.

Margaret believed that she had been kidnapped from her free black parents and her twin brother. She was adopted by Harriet, who claimed that Margaret was the daughter of her free black brother. But there is no record of a free black brother in the Ross family. More puzzling is the question of why Harriet, who spent so many years trying to reunite her own family, would kidnap a young girl from a free black family.

Was Margaret Stewart really Harriet's niece, or was she actually Tubman's daughter? Margaret was born in 1850—the same year that Harriet escaped. Some historians think that Harriet may have been desperate to escape because she was pregnant, and she did not want her child to be born into slavery. Harriet could have given birth on her way north, and left her baby in the care of a free black family. If the family had an infant, they could have passed Margaret off as his twin.

We will probably never know the true story of whether Margaret Stewart was rescued or kidnapped.

to bring her whole family together, Harriet must have been heartbroken. But since she was already on the Eastern Shore, she didn't want to waste the opportunity. Harriet found Stephen and Maria Ennals and their three children who were ready to go, and she agreed to take them north.

Snow and icy rain made this trip one of her most difficult, and the high price on Harriet's head meant they had to be even more careful. In order to avoid being detected by slave patrols that passed close by, the Ennals' baby was drugged with opium to keep it from crying. The children had no shoes to protect their little feet, and there was never enough food. At one point, Harriet brought the shivering and starving family to the home of a black man who was an Underground Railroad stationmaster. He didn't answer her secret knock on the door. Harriet knocked again. A white man opened the door and looked at Harriet suspiciously before telling her that her friend had been taken away for helping fugitive slaves. Tubman realized that she and all her passengers were in grave danger, so she rushed them away. She found a small island in the middle of a swamp on the edge of town. The group huddled in the wet grass all day long, cold, scared, and hungry, while Harriet prayed.

Snow and icy rain made the trip one of her most difficult, and the high price on Tubman's head meant they had to be even more careful.

No doubt alerted by the man who had answered the door, patrols searched nearby houses and fields for the fugitives. The Underground Railroad must have been alerted too, because at twilight, a man dressed in Quaker clothes passed close to the edge of the swamp. He seemed to be muttering to himself, but he

The Magee house in Canisteo, New York, was an Underground Railroad station used by escaping slaves on their way north.

was really giving Harriet instructions. He spoke just loud enough for her to hear. His wagon was in the barnyard of the next farm, he told her, and his horse was in the stable.

As soon as it got dark, Harriet crept to the farm. She hitched the horse to the wagon, which held food for the hungry fugitives, and went back for her passengers. Soon they were safely on their way to the next Underground Railroad depot.

The journey took a long time to complete, but eventually the Ennals family celebrated Christmas in Canada. It was Harriet's last rescue mission. She was exhausted, and many of her friends were worried about her safety.

The number of slaves Harriet Tubman led north is often exaggerated. Because the details of her rescues were kept

She returned to the South approximately thirteen times and rescued between seventy and eighty slaves.

secret, no one knows exactly how many trips she made or how many passengers she led to freedom. She returned to the South approximately thirteen times and rescued between seventy and eighty slaves. Another fifty or sixty more made their way to freedom using Tubman's careful directions.

Many years later, Harriet spoke her most famous words: "I was the conductor on the Underground Railroad for eight years, and I can say what most conductors can't say—I never ran my train off the track and I never lost a passenger."

Although Harriet stopped leading rescue missions, the Underground Railroad continued to operate for a few more years—until the slaves were freed during the Civil War. No other conductor came close to Harriet Tubman in leading so many slaves north.

Abraham Lincoln was elected president in November 1860. Shortly afterward, seven southern states seceded from the Union. Tubman believed that the country would soon be at war.

She was right. In April 1861 shots were fired at Fort Sumter in South Carolina. The Civil War had begun, and Harriet Tubman immediately thought about what she could do to help the Union and free the slaves.

Rebel soldiers stand beneath the Stars and Bars, the Confederate flag, at Fort Sumter on April 15, 1861, the day after the Union surrendered the fort.

CHAPTER 9

Raining Blood

When we came to get in the crops, it was dead men we reaped.

Tubman welcomed the war. Like most African Americans, she believed the war would bring an end to slavery. But President Lincoln entered the war without freeing the slaves, and while many people in the North were against slavery, they still believed that blacks were not the equal of whites. Northern blacks were not accepted into the Union army as soldiers.

Harriet was most concerned about the slave families trapped in the South. The Union navy captured two forts on the coast of South Carolina and set up a military zone called the Department of the South. It included parts of South Carolina, Georgia, and Florida. Fugitive slaves flooded in, seeking freedom. The governor of Massachusetts, John Andrews, asked Harriet to help.

Five generations on a plantation in South Carolina. Many families like the one in this 1862 photograph flooded into the Department of the South seeking freedom.

Once again, Harriet traveled back into slave territory, to Port Royal, South Carolina, from her home in Auburn, New York. She knew the risks were high, so Harriet said her good-byes to her family and friends, including Frederick Douglass, before she set out. She also asked her friends to take care of her parents during her absence.

Harriet Goes to War

In May 1862, a military ship, the *Atlantic*, transported Harriet to Beaufort, South Carolina. When she disembarked, she was greeted with chaos. Donations of clothes and food were coming in from the North, but had not been distributed yet. People who had spent their life in slavery had no idea how to work for wages—what to charge for their services, how to handle money, or even how to buy the things they needed.

Harriet was a natural leader, and she quickly took charge of the efforts to distribute clothes, food, books, and medicines to the Union soldiers and to the newly escaped slaves. Her role was never an official one, but the military officers were happy to have someone take control, and soldiers quickly learned that Harriet was the famous Underground Railroad conductor known as Moses. They tipped their hats whenever they met her.

Harriet built a washhouse where she taught the newly escaped African American women how to wash, sew, and bake for the Union soldiers, as a way of earning wages. She was able to draw food rations like other soldiers, but newly freed men and women wondered why Harriet had that privilege and they didn't. To avoid any hard feelings among them, Harriet gave up her rations. After that, the government never paid her a salary for the work she performed. And for the rest of the war, Harriet supported herself and her family by baking pies and making root

The 50th Pennsylvania Infantry soldiers shown here were among many at Beaufort, South Carolina, in 1862. Harriet supported herself by selling pies and root beer to the soldiers.

beer to sell to the soldiers. Whenever she had extra money, she sent it home to Auburn to her parents.

The cost of the war, both in terms of money and lives, was high. Harriet also worked as a nurse, and fought to keep soldiers alive in the face of outbreaks of contagious diseases like smallpox and measles.

The Emancipation Proclamation

The fact that Lincoln refused to free the slaves upset Harriet. How could the war be won without the support of blacks? "God won't let Master Lincoln beat the South till he does the right thing. Master Lincoln, he's a great man, and I am a poor negro, but the negro can tell Master Lincoln how to save the money and the young men. He can do it by setting the negroes free," she said.

In this undated illustration, Abraham Lincoln is shown reading a draft of the Emancipation Proclamation to his cabinet on July 22, 1862. In September it was announced to the world.

In September 1862 the Emancipation Proclamation was announced to the world. It was to take effect on January 1, 1863, and it granted freedom to all slaves in states still fighting against the Union, but Lincoln freed only the slaves in the Confederate states. This meant that slaves living in Union states were not made free by the Emancipation Proclamation. Maryland did not secede from the Union, so slavery was still legal in Harriet's birthplace.

Instead of celebrating the long-overdue Proclamation, Harriet became more directly involved in armed combat. She sneaked into enemy territory and gathered information for the Union. She even became an informal spymaster by sending out other ex-slaves as spies. Her efforts helped track Confederate movements in South Carolina. Harriet's experience leading slaves along the Underground Railroad served her well, and the North won more than one **guerrilla** operation because of the information she gathered. Harriet also followed troops into battle as a nurse, cook, and laundress.

The Combahee River Raid

The Emancipation Proclamation made it possible for black soldiers to join the Union forces from the South. So Harriet helped the Union recruit black soldiers from among the escaped slaves in Port Royal in order to form African American regiments. Then, on June 1, 1863, she became the first American woman to plan and lead a Civil War battle.

Working with Colonel James Montgomery and about three hundred black soldiers, Tubman guided three Union **gunboats** up the Combahee River in a sneak attack in the middle of the night. She stood in the lead boat with Montgomery while one of her spies, a local boatman, directed the ship around torpedoes planted below the river's surface. Union soldiers met little resistance as they made their way to the Confederate warehouses that Tubman's spy ring had discovered earlier. Once there, they took the food

The Emancipation Proclamation (shown above) was issued by Abraham Lincoln. The document was a milestone for African Americans, stating, "that all persons held as slaves...are and henceforth shall be free."

supplies and burned the crops and the weapons, making it harder for the Confederates to fight the war.

After the raid, overseers on nearby plantations tried to keep their slaves from running away. But when the slaves saw the Union gunboats returning to the base the next morning, they streamed from the fields and the riverbanks with everything they owned to board the ships. "I never saw such a sight . . ." Tubman later said. "Sometimes the women would come with twins hanging around their necks; it appears I never saw so many twins in my life; bags on their shoulders, baskets on their heads, and young ones tagging along behind, all loaded; pigs squealing, chickens screaming, young ones squealing."

Harriet was carrying two pigs for one of the fleeing slaves when the order "double quick" was given, which meant that they had to hurry up. "I started to run, stepped on my dress, it being

This etching from the July 14, 1863, edition of *Harpers Weekly* shows slaves streaming from the fields and riverbanks to board the Union gunboats after the Combahee River Raid.

Harriet's Bloomers

After ruining her clothes in the Combahee raid, Harriet changed her wardrobe. Women wearing pants were unheard of at the time, but suffragettes had recently begun wearing bloomers—loose-fitting trousers that combined the comfort of pants with the look of a dress. Suffragettes believed that equality with men might come sooner if their clothing allowed them to move around with the same ease as men. Harriet asked her friend to send a pair of bloomers for her to wear on future expeditions.

No doubt they made it easier for her to crawl behind enemy lines and gather information for the Union.

Named after their inventor, Amelia Jenks Bloomer, the new clothing choice attracted so much ridicule that they quickly fell out of fashion.

Harriet thought bloomers like these would allow her to move about more freely on her spy and combat missions.

rather long, and fell and tore it almost off, so that when I got on board the boat, there was hardly anything left of it but shreds," Harriet wrote to a friend.

The Combahee River raid not only destroyed valuable Confederate supplies, it also freed more than 750 slaves. Harriet's heroism was written about in newspapers in the North. It was the first time that the name Harriet Tubman was mentioned in print. It was finally revealed that she and the famous Underground Railroad conductor known as Moses were the same person.

The Fifty-Fourth Massachusetts Voluntary Infantry

Harriet's raid helped prove that black soldiers were a brave and powerful fighting force. One of the most famous black regiments was the Fifty-Fourth Massachusetts, under the command of a white abolitionist named Robert Gould Shaw. The regiment included two of Frederick Douglass's sons and Sojourner Truth's grandson. The 650 men of the Fifty-Fourth arrived in South Carolina the day after the Combahee raid.

The Fifty-Fourth was one of the regiments ordered to take part in an assault on South Carolina's Fort Wagner on July 17, 1863. Harriet followed them up the coast as a nurse and a cook, and may have done some scouting along the way. She served Colonel Shaw his breakfast before he went off to battle at Fort Wagner. It would be his last meal.

Tubman worked day and night nursing the sick and wounded men. . .

Harriet compared the battle to a raging storm. "And then we saw the lightning, and that was the guns; and then we heard the thunder, and that was the big guns; and then we heard the rain falling, and that was the drops of blood falling; and when we came to get in the crops, it was dead men we reaped."

This memorial to Robert Gould Shaw and the black soldiers of the 54th Massachusetts Voluntary Regiment was dedicated on Boston Commons in 1897.

The North knew that Fort Wagner would be almost impossible to take and the assault was a terrible failure. The Fifty-Fourth proved their worth that day. No one could say that black soldiers were not as brave or as strong as white soldiers. But they paid a terrible price: almost forty percent of the regiment's men

The courage of the men of the Fifty-Fourth proved that black soldiers were as strong and daring as white soldiers. This 1890 painting, *The Storming of Fort Wagner*, celebrates their bravery.

were dead or wounded. All together, the Union lost 1,515 soldiers at Fort Wagner; the Confederates lost only 174 men.

Harriet worked day and night nursing the sick and wounded men while also trying to support herself by baking in between hospital shifts. She was exhausted and finally took a leave from her duties in the fall of 1863. She hadn't seen her parents in a year and half, so she returned to Auburn to see them.

In 1864, Harriet was in Boston and met Sojourner Truth, the famous preacher and abolitionist. At that time, she and Tubman were probably the most famous black women in the nation.

Sojourner Truth (1797–1883)

Isabella Baumfree was born a slave in New York State around 1797. Like Harriet, she was "rented" to other farmers by her owner. She was sold many times. When her last owner refused to free her as he had promised, Baumfree took matters into her own hands and freed herself by running away. She moved to New York City and attended Methodist and African Methodist Episcopal Zion churches. By 1843 she had changed her name to Sojourner Truth, and traveled throughout the North as a preacher and an abolitionist.

Sojourner Truth, shown in this c. 1864 photograph, was a runaway slave who became a famous abolitionist and preacher.

Although they respected each other, they disagreed about President Lincoln. Truth was making speeches to help Lincoln get reelected, but Harriet was not interested in helping the president. She was unhappy with the treatment that black soldiers received. "We colored people didn't understand then he was our friend. All we knew was that the first colored troops sent south from Massachusetts only got seven dollars a month, while the white regiments got fifteen. We didn't like that."

Truth invited Harriet to join her on a visit to Washington, where she intended to meet Lincoln in person, but Harriet refused. Harriet later learned that Lincoln had been very kind to Truth at their meeting. "I'se sorry now I didn't see Master Lincoln and thank him," Harriet said, many years later.

Harriet returned to her nursing duties for the remainder of the war.

The South Surrenders

Finally, on April 9, 1865, Confederate General Robert E. Lee surrendered and the war was over. Harriet celebrated with the rest of the country, but just five days later President Lincoln was shot. Lincoln's secretary of state and Harriet's good friend, William H. Seward, was wounded in a different assassination attempt that same night.

This 1865 lithograph by Currier & Ives depicts John Wilkes Booth shooting President Lincoln at Ford's Theater on April 4, 1865.

When the war ended, Harriet was approximately forty-three years old. Slavery, the thing she had fought against ever since she was a little girl, when she first ran away and hid in a pigsty, was finally abolished. And although she may have wanted to rest, there was still work to be done. Harriet stayed in the South for the next few months taking care of African American soldiers. She did her job as well as the white nurses but was not treated equally. Black soldiers were kept in separate, inferior hospitals, and Harriet, who was not paid, had to scramble for supplies for the black patients. That experience taught her that there were still many injustices in the world, and she would fight against them for the rest of her life.

CHAPTER 10

More Battles to Fight

"Come hustle out of here! We don't carry niggers for half-fare."
—New Jersey train conductor

After the war ended, Harriet Tubman eventually moved to the Colored Hospital at Fort Monroe, Virginia. She grew more and more upset about the fact that black soldiers did not receive the same treatment as whites. African American soldiers were more than twice as likely to die in the hospital as their white counterparts. Not

This 1862 wood engraving shows wounded black soldiers being treated and sent to the hospital at Fort Monroe, where, Harriet complained, they did not get the same level of care as white soldiers.

surprisingly, Harriet tried to do something about it.

She traveled to Washington, D.C., and spoke to Secretary of State William Seward. He put her in touch with the U.S. Surgeon General, who promised to appoint Harriet "Nurse or Matron" of the black hospital at Fort Monroe, Virginia, and to send supplies. She also applied for back pay from the U.S. government, for all her years of service as a scout, a spy, and a nurse during the war.

African Americans still faced racism after winning their freedom in the Civil War. This print shows a well-dressed black man being forced to leave a railway car by a train conductor.

The appointment and the supplies never arrived, and Harriet's petition for back pay got lost in the Washington **bureaucracy**. As summer wore on, she realized that she had to return to her parents in Auburn. She had struggled to send them money during the war years. They were totally dependent upon her, and she needed more money than she could earn by selling pies in order to support them. In October 1865 she traveled home.

On this trip from Virginia to Auburn, New York, Harriet experienced firsthand the **racism** that the war could not abolish. She was a war hero, but a train conductor in New Jersey tried to force her to ride in the baggage car. He believed that Harriet's

Winning Citizenship

In January 1865, Congress had passed the Thirteenth **Amendment** abolishing slavery, but African Americans were still not full citizens of the United States, and they still did not have the right to vote. The Fourteenth Amendment, ratified, or formally approved by a majority of the states, in 1868, overturned the Dred Scott case and made African Americans full citizens. Southern states were required to ratify the amendment before they were readmitted to the Union. Two years later, the Fifteenth Amendment was ratified, which gave all male citizens the right to vote regardless of race or color.

Even though discrimination against African American men was now illegal, the former Confederate states quickly developed many ways to keep blacks from voting in the South by passing laws that required men to be able to read and write, own property, or pay a high tax in order to vote. The requirements were out of reach for most black men, especially for former slaves.

After winning citizenship, black men were free to vote. This 1867 woodcut shows black citizens voting for the first time. Southern states quickly passed laws to keep blacks from voting.

soldier's pass for a half-fare train ticket was stolen or forged. She explained politely that she worked for the government and could ride wherever she liked, but he shouted, "Come hustle out of here! We don't carry niggers for half-fare."

Harriet refused to move. He tried to force her, and she resisted. Eventually it took four men to wrestle Harriet out of her seat. Her arm was broken in the process, and she was dumped in the baggage car for the rest of the trip. No one came to her aid, and some passengers even suggested that the conductor throw her off the moving train.

Struggles in Auburn

Harriet arrived home safely in Auburn, New York, but the winter was a hard one. In addition to her parents, a number of other relatives lived in her small home. Harriet's injuries prevented her from working for the next few months, and they had to burn their fences for firewood.

Harriet's mother had to go without her tobacco and tea, and she complained often. One day, Harriet got so upset that she shut herself up in her closet for some peace and quiet. She always trusted God to provide for her, and she probably prayed. When she came out, she told her niece to put a large pot on the stove. "We're going to have soup today," she said. Then she grabbed a basket and walked to the market.

Harriet's injuries prevented her from working for the next few months, and they had to burn their fences for firewood.

Harriet walked from stall to stall with her empty basket. A butcher offered her a soup bone and told her to pay him when she could. Soon, other vendors did the same. Harriet went home with a full basket, and her family did not go to bed hungry that night. Harriet hated taking charity for herself, but she always did whatever it took to take care of her family.

Even though the family struggled for the next few years, Harriet's small house was always full of friends, family, boarders, and others who were passing through Auburn. Keeping everyone fed and clothed was a constant struggle, but no one in need was turned away from Harriet's doorstep.

Harriet Tubman's Biography

Despite her own needs, Harriet continued to raise funds for various freedmen's charities. She organized fairs and raised several hundred dollars over the next couple of years. Her petition for back pay from the government for her years of work as a scout and nurse was ignored in Washington. Finally, Harriet decided to publish a book about her life in order to raise money.

Sarah Bradford, a white abolitionist who lived in Auburn, had written many letters for Ben and Rit to send to Harriet while she was away at war. When Harriet returned home, she and Sarah became great friends.

Harriet's friends agreed to pay for someone to write a biography about her, and they chose Bradford to do it.

Harriet Tubman wears her Civil War garb in this engraving created for *Scenes in the Life of Harriet Tubman*.

Bradford interviewed Harriet and contacted prominent abolitionist leaders for stories about Tubman's heroism. *Scenes in the Life of Harriet Tubman* was rushed into print in December 1868. Unfortunately, the book was somewhat incomplete and told only half of Harriet's exciting life story; it also contained many mistakes. But it made much-needed money for Harriet's family.

Harriet Remarries

In October 1867, Harriet learned that John Tubman had been murdered in Maryland. Violence against blacks in the South was on the rise after the war, and John Tubman was one of its victims. She and John did not have any communication since the day she learned about his new wife. If she grieved for him, she did so privately. It is possible that Harriet believed in the wedding vow "till death do us part," because she never talked about marrying again until after John's death.

One of Harriet's boarders was a former soldier named Nelson Davis. He had a job at a brickyard and was sick with **tuberculosis**. Davis was twenty-five and Harriet was at least twenty years older. Not much is known about their courtship, but Harriet's friends believed she was in

Photographed in 1887 or 1888, Nelson Davis sits by the barn at Harriet's home in Auburn.

love. On March 18, 1869, they were married at the Central Presbyterian Church in Auburn. Harriet's family, along with many of her powerful white friends, attended the ceremony.

The next year, Harriet and Nelson started a brick-making business on her property, but the brickyard turned out to be bad for Harriet's crops: The water needed to make the bricks flooded her garden. She had to call on friends for charity again. Nelson was often sick, so Harriet continued to bear the burden of feeding the entire household.

A Gold Swindle

That heavy responsibility to care for her family may have been the reason why Harriet's famous sixth sense for avoiding danger failed her. In 1873, two black men arrived in Auburn and approached Harriet's brother John Henry Stewart, claiming they had a trunk full of gold coins worth $5,000 that they had smuggled from South Carolina. The men said they couldn't be seen with the gold and would trade it for $2,000.

Harriet heard stories about Southerners burying their gold during the war, and that it was their slaves who had done the digging. She believed the men and talked a white friend into giving her $2,000 in paper money in exchange for a share of the profits.

Harriet heard stories about Southerners burying their gold during the war, and that it was their slaves who had done the digging.

When Harriet, along with her brother, husband, and the white friend, arrived at the meeting place with the money, the two men managed to separate her from the others. They led her into the woods where they claimed the chest

Buried Confederate Gold

Millions of dollars in gold was said to have been lost during and after the Civil War—buried by individual plantation owners and even by the Confederate government to keep it out of the hands of the Union. Thirty million dollars may have been buried outside of Savannah, Georgia. Treasure hunters and historians have tried to find the gold for years, but it has never been located.

Men searched for hidden Confederate gold all over the South after the Civil War ended, as depicted in this 1878 print.

was hidden. Harriet soon realized that something was wrong. But it was too late. The men either drugged her or knocked her out.

Harriet's friends waited and worried, and finally they went searching for her in the woods. They found her the next morning bound and gagged. The chest was full of rocks and the $2,000 was gone.

This portrait of Harriet Tubman was taken between 1860 and 1875.

More Setbacks

Money continued to be Harriet's biggest worry for the rest of the 1870s and 1880s. It sometimes seemed as if she was visited by one setback after another, but she never gave up. She and Nelson separated the farm from the brickyard and managed them both, and she continued to take in anyone who needed help. In 1874 they adopted a baby girl named Gertie.

Harriet's father never met this grandchild, having died in 1871 in his mid-eighties. Harriet's mother lived until 1880. She was never reunited with the daughters who had been sold, but she and her husband spent many years in freedom, surrounded by their children, grandchildren, and great-grandchildren.

It sometimes seemed as if she was visited by one setback after another, but she never gave up.

Sometime after Rit's death, Harriet's farmhouse burned down. She built a brick house in its place. By this time, her husband was very ill, and her nephew John Henry Stewart died, leaving Harriet with his wife, Eliza, and their three small children to care for. Harriet's own headaches and seizures continued to trouble her health, and, as always, there was never enough money.

Tubman's fame as an Underground Railroad conductor and a Civil War hero had faded, and her petition for back pay continued to be stalled by government bureaucracy. Although many of Harriet's friends had helped her contact the government and fill out the complicated paperwork, her application seemed to get sidetracked at every turn. Harriet asked Sarah Bradford to reissue her biography.

Almost twenty years had passed since the book was first published. Racism had been on the rise since the end of the war. In the push to reunite the North and South, many Americans glorified the South's "Lost Cause" and tried to make slavery seem less harsh than it had really been. If the book was going to sell as many copies as Harriet hoped, a new version was necessary. *Harriet, the Moses of Her People*, published in 1886, painted a milder picture of life in slavery. Some of Harriet's stories, like her escape to the pigsty when she was a little girl, were exaggerated to make them seem funny instead of tragic.

Harriet seems to have enjoyed her fame, and now that she was a public figure for the second time, people wanted to hear her speak.

There is no record of how Harriet felt about this new slant on her biography, but the new book raised the money she was so desperate for, and brought her

The title page of *Harriet, the Moses of Her People*. In this second biography, many of Harriet's childhood stories were made comical instead of depicting the real cruelties of slavery.

HARRIET

THE MOSES OF HER PEOPLE

BY

SARAH H. BRADFORD

"Farewell, ole Marster, don't think hard of me, I'm going on to Canada, where all de slaves are free."

"Jesus, Jesus will go wid you, He will lead you to His throne, He who died has gone before you, Trod de wine-press all alone."

NEW YORK
PRINTED BY
J. J. LITTLE & CO.
1901

Elizabeth Cady Stanton addressed the first Women's Rights Convention in Seneca Falls, New York, on June 20, 1848. Harriet fought to win women the right to vote.

name to the public's attention once again. Harriet seems to have enjoyed her fame, and now that she was a public figure for the second time, people wanted to hear her speak.

She had always believed that women should have the right to vote, so she joined the fight to win the vote for women. She began appearing at women's suffrage meetings and telling her stories. The rest of her life would be devoted to the cause of women's right to vote. And she also wanted to open a home and hospital for the elderly and the poor.

CHAPTER 11

The Last Years

[Women] were on the scene to administer to the injured, to bind up their wounds and tend them through weary months of suffering in army hospitals. If those deeds do not place woman as man's equal, what do?

In 1870, African American men were granted the right to vote, but women, white or black, were still not allowed to vote. Harriet was old friends with many leaders of the women's suffrage movement, including Susan B. Anthony and Elizabeth Cady Stanton. During the 1880s and 1890s, Harriet spoke at women's suffrage meetings in New York and Boston whenever she could.

Elizabeth Cady Stanton (seated) and Susan B. Anthony were two leaders of the women's suffrage movement. Harriet was friends with both women and supported their cause.

Working for Women's Equality

Even as she grew older and frailer, Harriet's stories captured her audience. More than once, her appearance onstage was the most exciting moment of a convention. Harriet talked about her war years and the other women who "were on the scene to administer to the injured, to bind up their wounds and tend them through weary months of suffering in army hospitals. If those deeds do not place woman as man's equal, what do?" she would ask.

Harriet never learned to read, so train schedules were of little use to her. When she would want to go somewhere, she would simply go to the depot and wait until a train was going in the right direction and then get on it.

The suffrage meetings Harriet traveled to were **integrated**—both blacks and whites were welcome. But that wasn't always true of hotels. Once, when Harriet was scheduled to speak at a convention

More than once, her appearance onstage was the most exciting moment of a convention.

in Rochester, New York, she slept sitting up in a train station. She had no other place to go and was too proud to ask her friends for help. From then on, her friends made sure that Harriet was invited to spend the night in someone's home.

A Constant Worry Over Money

Even though Harriet had a busy public life, there was sadness at home. Her husband, Nelson Davis, died on October 18, 1888, probably of tuberculosis. He was just forty-five years old. Harriet was close to seventy, and she still had a large group of people depending on her for support—young and old, black

Tubman's Back Pay

In 2002, a group of middle-school students from Albany, New York, visited the Harriet Tubman Home in Auburn. When they learned that Harriet had never received her back pay, they were outraged. They wrote a letter to and later met with Senator Hillary Rodham Clinton. In 2003, Congress finally voted to provide Tubman with some of her back pay. A check for $11,750 was sent to the Harriet Tubman Home for the museum and the library.

In 2003, Congress finally voted to provide Harriet with her back pay.

and white, and all poorer than she was. She didn't have time to mourn her husband; she had to keep food on the table.

Harriet's application for back pay was still stalled in Congress. "You wouldn't think that after I served the flag so faithfully I should come to want under its folds," she said. In June 1890, Congress passed a law giving small pensions to widows of war veterans, and Harriet filed a claim the next month. Nelson Davis had changed his name after the war, and applying for the pension was a long and complicated process for Harriet. Five years later, she was finally granted a widow's pension of eight dollars a month.

Two years after that, a New York congressman tried once again to win Harriet the pay and recognition she deserved. The government never gave Tubman her back pay or acknowledged her work as a scout, but after two years of negotiations, in 1899, Congress increased her pension to twenty dollars a month. Twelve dollars were for her work as a nurse. By now, Harriet was almost eighty years old.

Harriet was an active member of the AME Zion Church in Auburn and she raised money for needy families. She dreamed of opening a home for poor and elderly African Americans. In 1896, she had successfully bid on a piece of property next to her farm with the help of friends and a $1,000 mortgage. Until she could raise the money to build a separate home for the poor, her own home continued to be a place where anyone in need was welcomed.

Terrible headaches continued to trouble Harriet. When it seemed as if she couldn't take the pain anymore, she had brain surgery at Massachusetts General Hospital in the late 1890s. A friend reported that

An 1895 photograph of Harriet Tubman. The scar from her childhood head injury is still visible.

Harriet refused to take drugs to make her sleep during the operation. She asked for a bullet to bite down on, like the Civil War soldiers she had nursed through amputations. She said prayers throughout the operation. Afterward, she seemed to have less pain.

Harriet recovered from the operation, but she was never able to raise the funds to start her home for the elderly. Her small pension was never enough. One year she had to sell her cows to pay the taxes on the property. In 1903 she gave the property to the AME Zion Church hoping that it would build the home she had long dreamed of.

The Harriet Tubman Home

The Harriet Tubman Home for the Aged and Infirm Negroes finally opened its doors in 1908, but Harriet was upset by some of the church's policies. Residents were charged $150 to live

The Harriet Tubman Home for the Aged opened its doors in 1908.

there, even though Harriet had wanted the home to be accessible to anyone—especially those people who didn't have $150. She knocked on doors and asked for donations for the poor people who couldn't afford the charges.

By 1910, traveling, speaking, and fund-raising were too much for Harriet. She was close to ninety years old and in a wheelchair, but she hadn't lost her spirit. Margaret Stewart's daughter Alice remembered the day when she was a little girl

This last known photograph of Harriet Tubman was taken in 1911. Her spirit was strong until the very end of her life.

picking flowers in a field while her mother visited with Aunt Harriet. Suddenly Alice realized that something was coming toward her. Harriet had slipped out of her wheelchair and silently slithered through the grass on her stomach to surprise the little Alice. She told Alice that she had often used the same trick to sneak by Confederate guards during the war. To them she was nothing more than a shadow.

The next year Harriet had to move out of her own house and into the Harriet Tubman Home. Her spirit was still joyful, but her body had started to give out. Shortly before she died, she looked at her family members and friends who gathered by her bedside and said, "I go away to prepare a place for you." She died of pneumonia on March 10, 1913.

People still leave flowers at Harriet Tubman's grave site in Auburn, New York.

Military Honors

Harriet was buried next to her brother in Fort Hill Cemetery in Auburn with military honors. On June 14, 1914, a large bronze plaque was placed at the Cayuga County Courthouse that read: "Called the 'Moses' of her people, during the Civil War, with rare courage, she led over three hundred Negroes up from slavery to freedom, and rendered invaluable service as nurse and spy." Booker T. Washington, the most prominent black leader of the day, was the speaker at its unveiling.

Harriet Tubman has since received many honors. Many museums in the South are named for her. Eleanor Roosevelt, the wife of President Franklin Delano Roosevelt, christened a ship the *Harriet Tubman* in 1944, and commemorative postage stamps were printed with her image in 1978 and 1995.

But honors weren't important to Harriet—freedom was. She embraced the American ideals of liberty and justice for all people, and she showed the world that one person could make a difference. She inspired countless others to fight for their freedom and their rights and to help those in need.

There are many facts about Harriet's life that are lost to history, such as the details of her Underground Railroad trips and her spy missions for the Union. But what is clear is that Harriet Tubman was a freedom fighter who never surrendered and who was a true American hero.

This 1978 U.S. postage stamp commemorates Harriet Tubman's role as a conductor on the Underground Railroad.

Glossary

abolitionists—people who were in favor of ending slavery.

amendment—a change, addition, or correction to the Constitution.

auction—a sale of property to the highest bidder.

bureaucracy—complicated procedures with many formal rules.

corncrib—a bin for storing ears of corn.

Deep South—southeast region of United States that includes, in part, Alabama, Georgia, Louisiana, North Carolina, and South Carolina.

Eastern Shore—a region in Maryland on the east side of Chesapeake Bay.

Emancipation Proclamation—the announcement by President Abraham Lincoln in 1862 that all slaves in the Confederate states were free.

fugitives—runaway slaves, especially those who went into hiding.

guerrilla—an act of sabotage or harassment led by a small unit of soldiers against the enemy.

gunboats—small, fast ships with guns, used in rivers and shallow waters.

gunnysacks—sacks made of coarse, rough fabric used for storing grain.

handbills—posters, often delivered by hand and displayed in places where people would see them.

integrated—including people of all races and both genders.

intuition—the ability to know or sense information by instinct.

lawsuit—a claim brought to a court of law.

meteor shower—a group of small particles in the solar system that produce streaks of light when they enter the earth's atmosphere.

militia—an organized group of citizens acting as a military or police force.

North Star—a bright star in the northern hemisphere that roughly marks the North Pole.

overseer—a supervisor, or boss. Slave owners often put overseers in charge of their slaves.

plantations—large farms or group of farms.

prejudice—a dislike of a person or a group of people based on an unjust reason, such as the color of their skin.

racism—the belief that members of a particular race are different or inferior.

recruits—newcomers to a group, such as the army.

refugees—people who flee, or run away from their home to get to a safer place. Slaves living in the North and in Canada were considered to be refugees.

safe houses—places where fleeing slaves could seek rest and safety.

slaveholders—people who owned slaves.

suffragette—a woman who fought for women's right to vote.

treason—the crime of betraying one's country.

tuberculosis—a lung disease that killed many people in the 1800s.

visions—things seen in a dream or in a trance.

Bibliography

Books

Bordewich, Fergus M. *Bound for Canaan: The Epic Story of the Underground Railroad, America's First Civil Rights Movement.* New York: Amistead, 2005.

Bradford, Sarah H. *Harriet, The Moses of Her People.* Bedford, Mass.: Applewood Books, 2003.

Clinton, Catherine. *Harriet Tubman: The Road to Freedom.* New York: Little, Brown and Company, 2004.

Hansen, Joyce, and Gary McGowan. *Freedom Roads: Searching for the Underground Railroad.* Chicago: Cricket Books, 2003.

Haskins, Jim. *Get on Board: The Story of the Underground Railroad.* New York: Scholastic Inc., 1993.

Humez, Jean M. *Harriet Tubman: The Life and the Life Stories.* Madison, Wisc.: University of Wisconsin Press, 2003.

Larson, Kate Clifford. *Bound for the Promised Land: Harriet Tubman.* New York: Ballantine Books, 2004.

Articles

Slackman, Michael. "In Search of Back Pay for Heroine of Civil War." *The New York Times* (November 1, 2003): B1.

Documentaries

American Experience: Roots of Resistance: A Story of the Underground Railroad. PBS Video, 1990.

History Channel Presents: The Underground Railroad. A&E Television Networks, 1999.

Web Sites

Harriet Tubman Historical Society: www.harriettubman.com

National Geographic.com: The Underground Railroad:
    www.nationalgeographic.com/railroad/j2.html
National Park Service: Harriet Tubman Special Resource Study:
    www.harriettubmanstudy.org
New York History Net: www.nyhistory.com/harriettubman/life.htm

Image Credits

About the Author

Laurie Calkhoven is the author of many nonfiction books for young
people, including *George Washington: An American Life*. She lives in New
York City.

Index